W9-AXA-415

WHILE WE RUN THIS RACE

WHILE WE RUN
THIS RACE

Confronting the Power of Racism
in a Southern Church

Nibs Stroupe
and Inez Fleming

ORBIS BOOKS

Maryknoll, New York 10545

The Catholic Foreign Mission Society of America (Maryknoll) recruits and trains people for overseas missionary service. Through Orbis Books, Maryknoll aims to foster the international dialogue that is essential to mission. The books published, however, reflect the opinions of their authors and are not meant to represent the official position of the society.

Copyright © 1995 by Nibs Stroupe and Inez Fleming

All rights reserved. No part of this publication may be reproduced or transmitted in any form or by any means, electronic or mechanical, including photocopying, recording or any information storage or retrieval system, without prior permission in writing from the publishers.

Queries regarding rights and permissions should be addressed to: Orbis Books, P. O. Box 308, Maryknoll, New York 10545-0308.

Published by Orbis Books, Maryknoll, NY 10545-0308
Manufactured in the United States of America

Library of Congress Cataloging-in-Publication Data

Stroupe, Nibs
    While we run this race : confronting the power of racism in a
southern church / Nibs Stroupe and Inez Fleming.
      p.   cm.
   ISBN 1-57075-000-9 (pbk.)
    1. Race relations—Religious aspects—Presbyterian Church.
2. Oakhurst Presbyterian Church (Decatur, Ga.) 3. Decatur (Ga.)—
Church history—20th century. 4. Georgia—Church history—20th
century. 5. Fleming, Inez. 6. Afro-American Presbyterians—
Georgia—Decatur—Biography. 7. Decatur (Ga.)—Race relations.
8. Georgia—Race relations. I. Fleming, Inez. II. Title
BX8949.D43S77   1995
261.8'348'009758225—dc20   95-5183
                                                CIP

"The diversity which we feared
has empowered us to confront
God's truth in the world."

Contents

Foreword   ix

Acknowledgments   xi

1. "The Journey Is Our Home"   1

2. "The Great Divide"   14

3. "I Have a Dream Today"   24

4. The American Nightmare   46

5. "Been in the Storm So Long"   68

6. "Seeing in a Mirror Dimly"—
   What It Means to Be White   90

7. "Come to the Waters"   107

8. "My Name Is Legion"   113

9. "We All . . . Everyone of Us"   130

10. "Many Streams, One River"   147

Recommended Readings   173

Foreword

Beneath the surface of the persuasive arguments in this important book lies a simple, powerful, and easily forgotten testimony, one that deserves our closest attention. For Nibs Stroupe, Inez Fleming, and their sisters and brothers at Oakhurst Presbyterian Church in an Atlanta suburb have dared to believe that the destructive powers of American racism can be challenged and transformed at the deepest human levels when we work together from the base of an informed, alternative, redemptive way of life. So it is important to remember that while these pages are filled with powerful words that expose and deny the claims of white racism, the book is most important to us because its greatest gift is based on much more than words. At its best the work emerges from the costly, lived experiences of a multiracial gathering of Christian believers who are painfully, joyfully struggling to find a way to take seriously both the promise and the perils of racial identity without forgetting their deepest identity as children of the living God and followers of the Christ who called us to let His love for us and our love for each other shatter old boundaries and create new communities.

In this work, written primarily by Nibs, the continuing life of the Oakhurst church community plays a secondary role to his valuable, penetrating analysis of white American racism and its demonic powers. Still, while we wait for the story of the church to emerge more fully at some later date from the hearts and minds of Nibs, Inez, and the others, we have much reason to rejoice now in the courage, commitment, and insight of this child of white southern patriarchy. For his willingness to take risks in his writing and in his living lends an authentic vitality to his urgent call for us to confront and overcome the deeply entrenched power of racism wherever we find it, beginning—as he does—within our own hearts, but always reaching beyond our personal lives to the institutions that make up our wounded churches, communities, and nation.

At the same moment, we must surely give thanks for the fact that Nibs has Inez as sister, teacher, companion, and friend to help him and Oakhurst. For in these perilous and often discouraging times we need them all. We need them to challenge and encourage us, to remind us that the struggle for new communities of hope will certainly intensify as we open ourselves beyond the older bi-polar black and white American racial categories to embrace the calling of our nation's expanding divine pluralism, as we encounter the growing divisiveness of economic disparities, and as we continue to confront the power of profit-driven American individualism.

In such a time we are grateful for all those who refuse to allow themselves to be squeezed into the mold of this world. We need them to work and pray, to study and sing with us while we run this magnificent and demanding race. We need them to remind us that unless the world of the loving God takes on its technicolored flesh in places like Decatur, Georgia, Denver, Colorado, and a thousand other points of hope, we might run this race in vain. And we certainly don't want to do that. So we give thanks for Nibs and Inez and all their family at Oakhurst. Holding and being held, we run with patience the race that takes us into the twenty-first century. Fortunately, they have written in a way that we can read while we run, continuing a great tradition, leaving us no excuses, offering magnificent possibilities of new life for our children and ourselves.

Vincent Harding
Denver, Colorado
Ash Wednesday, 1995

Acknowledgments

There are many people who helped to bring this book to fruition. I do not have space to name them all, but I do want to mention a few. First and foremost is my family, especially my mother, Mary Stroupe, and my wife, Caroline Leach, associate pastor at Oakhurst, and our children David and Susan.

I did the initial research and writing during a sabbatical funded by the Fund for Theological Education through Walter Schenk's office, after being nominated for the award by David Billings. I am grateful to Dr. Erskine Clarke of Columbia Theological Seminary and to Robert Evans of Plowshares Institute for providing great assistance in getting the manuscript to publishers. I am grateful to others who read the manuscript and provided helpful comments and criticism: Anne Womack, Ed Loring, David Billings, Moriba Karamoto, Harmon Wray, Martin Buss, and Vincent Harding.

I am especially grateful to Robert Ellsberg and Susan Perry of Orbis Books who have provided invaluable support and dialogue with me on the book and who have stayed with it when major revisions were done. I am grateful also to those who helped to prepare the manuscript in various stages: Rebecca Linafelt, Tim Beal, Kathleen Plate, Cheryl McKinzie, Angela Diamon, and Catherine Costello.

This book would not be possible without the support and life of Oakhurst Presbyterian Church. I am grateful to the members, elders, and friends of Oakhurst who have endured me and instructed me as pastor. I give thanks for the support of the Presbytery of Greater Atlanta, without whose continuing partnership there would be no Oakhurst. Most especially, I am grateful to Inez Fleming, who has invited me into her life in a way that few black people ever invite white people. She and the community of faith known as Oakhurst Presbyterian Church are the heart and soul of this book and our hope as a society as well.

CHAPTER 1

"The Journey Is Our Home"

This book has many sources, and I want to lift up two of them here. The first source is my identity as a white, Southern male who grew up in the 1950s and 1960s. For me and my Southern heritage, race was and is fundamental; it is more important than economic status, gender, religion, sexual orientation, or nationality. My observations of North American culture during my adult years have taught me that this central importance of race is not confined to the South but pervades our entire national life. Whereas other classifications of human beings may be more important on a global level, in North American culture, race is the most important. In spite of the gains of the civil rights movement, race remains fundamental. As a white Southerner, I am well aware of the dynamics of the centrality of race identity. I was raised on it.

The second source of this book is the multiracial church of which I am pastor: Oakhurst Presbyterian Church in Decatur, Georgia. Its current identity is a result of the movement of the city. Almost 30 years ago, it was an all-white church of eight hundred members. Then African-American people began to move into its neighborhood, and the transition began as we whites demonstrated our usual fear and flight in the presence

---

* From the song "Lead On, O Cloud of Yahweh," Ruth Duck, *Because We Are One People* (Chicago: Ecumenical Women's Centers, 1974).

of those people we call "black." In a few short years, Oakhurst became a church in crisis, as its membership plummeted over a decade to two hundred and down to eighty over the next decade. Yet, in the midst of the turmoil, some white people decided to stay in the church and some black people decided to come to the church. The long journey to health had begun with one giant step: white people and black people deciding to stay in the presence of one another. Our membership is now at 160.

As I write this, I have been pastor at Oakhurst for twelve years. Later, I will expand on the story of Oakhurst Presbyterian Church and on the possibilities it offers us for dealing with the centrality of race in our culture. Now, I want to lift up how much I have learned about the dynamics of race from the members and friends of this church who have struggled with me, confronted me, and celebrated with me. At times I have well understood why Andrew Hacker entitled his 1992 book *Two Nations: Black and White, Separate, Hostile, Unequal* (New York: Charles Scribner and Sons, 1992). The gulf between black and white in this culture seems so huge! I have also learned, however, that only when we acknowledge the power of this distance can we begin to build bridges over it. Though many problems remain for us at Oakhurst, we have begun to build these bridges by acknowledging the power of the system of race. We have done this by celebrating the vision that life is intended to be a tapestry of colors, not a race to see who will win. We have done this by risking to trust one another in a milieu that dictates that "trust" and "race" cannot abide together.

This book is about race. It is written in despair and hope. The source of the despair is the chasm between the races in this country. It is yet so deep and powerful, especially between those called "black" and those called "white." The great civil rights movement of thirty years ago has not produced the gains we all hoped it would. We still are a society divided by race, a society whose racial definitions are primary. People of darker color are still plagued by feelings of inadequacy and by a sense of injustice. Despite their accomplishments, scholarship, or national recognition, the power of race continues to grip them. Listen to the voice of African-American Henry Louis Gates, Jr., an internationally known scholar and professor at Harvard, in writing in *Loose Canons* about the pervasiveness of racism in his life:

> Even I—despite a highly visible presence as a faculty member at Cornell—have found it necessary to cross the street, hum a tune, or smile when confronting a lone white woman in a campus building or on the Commons late at night. (Once a white coed even felt it necessary to spring from an elevator that I was about to enter, in the very building where my department is housed.) Nor can I help but feel humiliation as I try to put a white person at ease in a dark place on campus at night, coming from nowhere, confronting that certain look of panic in his or her eyes, trying to think grand thoughts like Du Bois but—for the life of me—looking to him or her like Willie Horton. Grinning, singing, scratching my head, I have felt like Steppin Fetchit with a Ph.D. So much for Yale; so much for Cambridge (New York: Oxford University Press, 1992, pp. 135-36).

On the other side of the chasm, those of us called white are tired of race. Most of us believe that we have done enough to make the idea of equality a reality in this society. We made great shifts during the civil rights movement, and we continue to try to see all people as our equals. Yet, we continue to hear from people of darker color, especially African-American people, that racism is strong and is even growing. This is harsh news for us. It is a source of frustration and despair for white people.

Despair and resignation are not the only answers, however. There is hope of bridging this chasm. We did make progress in the civil rights movement, profound progress. Black people and white people did work together to make extraordinary changes in the government and institutional structures of our society. These same groups continue to seek to work together to ensure that the gains of the civil rights movement will not be eroded in a tide of racism. But we have not yet found the Promised Land, and often it seems as far away as ever. I am writing this book in the hope that it will take us closer to the Promised Land. The journey continues for all of us—indeed, the journey is our home.

We have had a glimpse of the Promised Land, a place where all people are seen and welcomed as the children of God, a place where God is the center of our lives. We all long to get to that place; but as we will see, we must yet travel through Esau's land, Gerasa, and many other places. We are still in the wilderness and will remain there for the foreseeable future, because we still are gripped by the power of the system of race. The most difficult step of all is the one that white people must take: to acknowledge the existence of this system of race. It is central to our society, but we white beneficiaries deny it even exists. We receive great benefits from it, and we operate in it daily.

Whenever I lead workshops on racism, I inevitably encounter many white people who despair. Their despair comes from gaining a glimpse of the great divide and participating in it. The temptation is to give in and give up because the power of race is so overwhelming. This temptation is strong for darker people also, for white resistance seems so deep and broad. And, the temptation to yield to racism remains strong. As we become aware of the power of race, our lives become more complicated. We encounter darker people who don't seem grateful for our efforts and white people who reject what we try to do. African Americans encounter white people who want to be showered with gratitude because they have taken a few, small steps against racism. The temptations to despair and resign oneself remain ever present.

Yet, there is also hope because the movement against the system of race is God's will for us. God is moving in our midst and asking us to join in the journey. There are more churches like Oakhurst in this society than we care to admit. As our culture gains more people of many skin colors and backgrounds, churches are responding to the diversity and the need to con-front the continuing power of race. The House of Bishops of the Episcopal Church passed a letter on the sin of racism, which was read in the pulpits of the denomination's churches on May 15, 1994. The 1994 Presbyterian General Assembly affirmed the need to struggle with racism as one of its six mission initiatives. These are signs of hope.

There are also personal stories—my story and those of Inez Fleming and others who have sought to begin bridging the great divide. While as individuals we are nothing to write home about, it is remarkable that we are able to struggle against the system of race together. Inez, an African American woman from Alabama who continues to struggle with the issue of whether to engage white people, has shared part of her life with me and invited me in. A white male Southerner who resisted the civil rights movement has heard that he must listen to other stories. We have been told, and we have believed, that we are enemies. And yet, through God's grace, through the church (of all places!), we have become friends.

In the midst of despair about the growing and continuing power of the system of race, these are signs of hope. The system of race is not inexorable, although it is powerful. In our time, we are asked to admit that it exists and to struggle against it. Although I have a long way to go, it should be clear that if I can begin to take a few steps against the system of race, anyone can. There is nothing magical about it, although it is miraculous. Because the process is so available, and yet so difficult to begin, I will list several steps we who claim the name white must take for hope to be born in our hearts and in this culture.

The first step is to admit that the system of race exists. I am not talking about acknowledging different races. I am talking about a *system* of race, a system of classifying people so that some gain access to opportunity and power while others are denied access. The system of race rewards those called white and penalizes those called black and other people of darker colors. Black people encounter the system daily. White people have pushed out of their consciousness.

In the spring of 1992, when the first verdict concerning the police officers who attacked Rodney King was announced, one of our white Oakhurst Church staff members was attending class at a local university in downtown Atlanta. A rebellion among young black people broke out in downtown Atlanta in response to the verdict. As the rebellion gathered steam and moved through downtown, our staff member decided to go out on the streets with the students to express solidarity with them, to express her anger and shock over the verdict. When she got out on the streets, however, she made a startling and difficult discovery: The black students were not interested in her political views. They did not care that she was in solidarity with them. They only cared about one thing: her racial classification. They saw that she was white, and they saw her as the enemy, as one who represented the injustice of the system of race. They did not care about her identity, her personal history, or her views on justice. They saw only the racial classification—she was white.

She was in danger. She perceived this, and before she could be harmed physically, she managed to get back into a school building while the storm of anger raged outside. She was not hurt physically, but she was hurt emotionally and spiritually. We talked about it at length after the incident. As we talked, her hurt and anger came out. Why were the black students mad at her? She was on their side. She, too, was greatly angered by the verdicts, but they didn't even take time to find that out. They just saw one thing: She was white. They didn't care about her as a person; they didn't care about her history of working for justice. She was hurt—she had been dehumanized.

As we searched for answers in a terrible situation, she began to discern that in the midst of great pain, she had been given a gift. For one brief moment, she had gained some insight into the power of racial classification. She had been given insight into what it means to be judged by race in this culture, to be judged first and foremost according to racial classification. Family history didn't matter. Political views were unimportant. A history of working for justice was irrelevant. The only thing that mattered was her racial classification. She discerned on a small scale what it means to be black in this culture. What had been an awful time could become a time with promise if she were willing to listen and gain from it. She discerned that she had experienced for a brief time what black people experience daily and constantly in this culture. The system of race does exist. Acknowledging that it exists is the first step for whites.

The second step people classified as white must take to build hope is to recognize the wide gap between whites and blacks and other people of darker color in this country. To survive the daily onslaught of the system of race, many people of darker color choose not to reveal their humanity in the presence of white people. This is a protective device to ward off feelings of hurt and anger that can arise when they encounter white people on any genuine level. Our white staff member discovered this unpleasant process when she experienced the system of race herself. To survive this process, many people of darker color maintain a distance between their personhood and their encounters with white people. We who are white often are slow to discern this distance because we do not have daily encounters with racism that tell us that we are not human, that our personal history and character do not count. Our daily encounter with the system of race tells us that we *do* count, that we are supposed to be in control.

We have difficulty discerning this distance between us and people of darker color because we do not believe that the system of race is so powerful. We are usually unaware that many people of darker color are always on guard in the presence of white people and generally do not want us involved in their lives.

This was demonstrated vividly in one of our earliest workshops. Inez Fleming was asking a white man about his African-American employees. He responded that he had shared information with them but that he could not tell what their reaction would be. She replied that that was because he was white. His reaction indicated that she might as well have walked over and slapped him in the face—she had insulted him by saying he did not understand because he was white. Although he called himself white, and was acting white, he somehow believed that he personally could transcend the system of race. He simply could not believe there was a reality in the black experience to which he did not have access. We who claim the name white are unwilling and often unable to admit how much the acceptance of our own category limits our ability to perceive and understand the experience of people of darker color.

We have run into this resistance in other workshops when white people wanted to equate their oppression as homosexuals or as women with that of people called black. At this point, we vigorously pressed our belief that while these types of oppression can open doors for understanding the condition of African-American people, they fail to enable white homosexuals or white women to fully grasp the vast gap created by the system of race.

The third step for us who are called white must take to build hope is to face our resistance honestly and forthrightly. I was reminded of this first line of white resistance on a national radio broadcast on June 21, 1993, that described Dr. Aaron Shirley, who runs a community health center in Jackson, Mississippi. The report gave some background information on Dr. Shirley because he had just won a MacArthur Foundation Genius Grant. The CNN reporter, Brian Cabell, stated that Dr. Shirley could sometimes be militant. The evidence cited for labeling Dr. Shirley as a militant was that he took pride in his people and his past. This description of Dr. Shirley indicates how threatened the system of race is when African-American people affirm their humanity—a term taken from the military is used to describe the affirmation of being black.

A second form of white resistance is to dismiss the particular black person discussing the system of race. Of course, one of the powers of racial classification is the belief that one person speaks for the whole group, i.e., that white people or black people are all alike. A healthy skepticism should be employed anytime a white or a black says she or he speaks for all whites or all blacks. The method we white people use, however, is often to seek other black people who will dispute discussions of the power of the system of race. If we can find them—and we usually can—then we dismiss any discussion of the power of race. In a perverse way, we accept for one brief moment the authority of a black person, but only because he or she ratifies *our* view of the power of race.

Whatever may be our particular source of resistance to hearing about the power of the system of race, we who are called white must seek to deepen our consciousness and listen to the voices that are able to break through our resistance. Like our white staff member, we must be willing to stay with the pain and hurt to discover and understand.

You who are white may be reading this now and wondering when I will discuss the responsibility of people of darker color for the system of race. All that we have heard thus far is "white this" and "white that." When do we hear about the darker people's responsibility for the system of race? When do darker people hear what they are supposed to do? If you are thinking in this manner, take heart. I, as a white man, now will seek with trepidation to introduce the discussion of the responsibilities of people of darker color, especially African-American people, in regard to the system of race.

First, African-Americans are asked to acknowledge their tendency toward dualism—one person in white society, one person with their people. It is a technique of survival, a process that frustrates white people because we do not want to understand the consequences of the system for people of darker color. It also makes life difficult for people of darker color, for they must be on guard in the presence of whites. They must learn, and they must teach, that white people are dangerous—especially when darker people affirm their humanity in the presence of white people. The world is a jungle and to survive the crazy, wild animals called white people, darker people must shrink in their humanity and be very cautious. Thus, for example, all African-American parents face a terrible and difficult dilemma concerning their children: When will they consciously come face-to-face with racism, and how will we teach them to cope with it? To teach them to deny the dualism and act as real persons in the presence of white people is to invite a dangerous white reaction. To teach them the dualism is to risk a shrinkage of their spirit and perpetuation of the system of race. It is a terrible dilemma, but it is real and must be acknowledged.

Second, darker people are asked to reflect on and acknowledge the extent to which they have accepted a white definition of themselves. This white definition includes the white lie that they can overcome racism by working hard, thus proving themselves worthy of white acceptance.

One of the blatant lies of the system of race is that those called black and other darker peoples can gain some measure of humanity by working hard and doing right. This way, the system of race shifts responsibility for oppression from the white people, who created it, to those it calls "non-white." The system of race thus posits that racism is the result not of white desire to maintain control, but rather of the "nonwhite" people's being inferior and less worthy. Racism, then, is not racism at all—it is the *natural* reaction of white people encountering those less than themselves. This is one of the damaging lies of the system of race.

This lie is damaging because it seeks to convince darker people that they are responsible for racism. If they worked hard and did right, then there would be no racism. This lie is damaging also because many darker people have accepted it and demeaned their own humanity. To accept this lie is to perpetuate the system of race and allow those who have claimed the name white to be absolved of responsibility for it. The most damaging part of this lie is that it assists in stripping darker people of the human dignity endowed them by God. The lie must be acknowledged, confronted, and challenged.

This is not to say that darker people should not work hard. They should and do. It is to say that the hard work must be directed toward affirming their humanity and their culture in the public arena, rather than toward convincing white people of their worthiness. The dualism and the acceptance of the white lie produce great anger, tension, and dissonance; darker people are asked to find constructive ways to channel and express that anger and tension.

Violence in the African-American community, which the media love to emphasize and which scares white people, is rooted in the tension and rage that result from racism. This observation does not seek to equate racism with violence or to absolve the black community from responsibility for the violence. Yet, racism is the significant factor in the rage and violence. The failure to recognize it as a primary factor in the violence puts our entire society in great peril.

Finally, darker people are asked to resist the temptations of separatism and segregation. It must be recognized that to survive their perilous journey, they must return to their culture and draw from the waters of their people. As one of our African-American members put it, "I must get back with just my people, without any of ya'll around—just to survive my entry into the white world." This statement is not separatist or hostile—it simply recognizes the continuing power of race.

The temptations to separatism and segregation are great because it is so difficult to get white people to acknowledge the humanity of darker people. The tendency, then, is to return to the old dualism in which authentic encounters with white people are as limited as possible. The extreme form of this tendency is separation, in which total withdrawal from white society is sought. This may be helpful in the short run, but in the long run, it only enhances the system of race because segregation is what most white people want anyway. Historically, the separatism movement in the African-American community has gone in tandem with an increase in white control of the institutions of society.

Darker people are damned if they do and damned if they don't. That is the terrible power of the system of race, and it is the reason that darker people have so few viable options. Yet, I (a white male) urge them to "do," to affirm their humanity in the presence of whites, to shift from accepting our definition to demanding a change in the definition. Such a shift requires great courage, ingenuity, and endurance.

"We who believe in freedom cannot rest." That line from a song written by Bernice Johnson Reagon of Sweet Honey in the Rock describes our journey together in the land of the system of race. I do not mean to imply that there can be no sabbaths, no sabbaticals, no rest. In a culture that defines life by labor and consumption, it is a revolutionary act to rest. Perhaps a better line would be: "We who believe in freedom *must* rest."

So, do not hear my use of the theme of "Ella's Song" as another ode to being a workaholic! Hear it this way: The song is based on the life of Ella Baker, one of the great organizers of the civil rights movement. She was a field secretary early on with the Southern Christian Leadership Conference, and she believed that the key to the movement was the organizing of young people. She urged youth not to focus on themselves, but on the movement. She urged us all to begin the journey. Her story is told by Bernice Johnson Reagon in *We Who Believe in Freedom* (New York: Anchor Books, 1993). The song reminds us that the system of race is ever present and that our awareness of it must be present also. The journey is our home; and like Moses, we may not get to the Promised Land, but we must be on our way.

The system of race continues to grip us with astonishing power. Is it inexorable? I would not write this book if I felt it was inevitable and unstoppable. It is powerful, but it is not omnipotent. All of us—whatever our racial classification—are asked to reexamine our complicity and participation in the system of race. We must begin with a review of our own lives, not to feel guilt or anger, but to be realistic about encountering the power of racism. It is only through a realistic encounter with the roots of racism that the seeds of hope can be born. That is what this books means. That is what I, as its author, intend.

Of course, the author of a book may be the worst interpreter of its meaning. I can put my intentions in writing, but many other voices speak in my writing and through it, including those of readers and critics—even my own, although I may not be consciously aware of them. In workshops, speeches, and conversations, I already have seen some reactions to my approach. People classified as white often believe I have vastly overrated the power of race and am unnecessarily singling out white people for responsibility and being a divisive force when conciliation is needed. Those classified as darker people often believe I am arrogant in seeking to describe their journeys; that I am too soft on black people, especially in assigning responsibility for the well-publicized ills of the black community; that I am a white person riddled with guilt where race is concerned.

All of those reactions may have merit, but I still maintain that the continuing power of the system of race is vastly underrated in this culture, to the detriment of all of us. I have attempted to place it in proper perspective, but if you believe that I am off the mark or have overrated it, please do not dismiss it entirely. It is vital to our future vision as a people that we seek to eradicate the power of the system of race.

Finally, let us remember that God has not given up on us, that in the midst of stubborn resistance, in the midst of resignation and despair, God comes to redeem us and call us into new life. God's redeeming and renewing activity is our source of hope. In a world that seems crazy over race, God reminds us that the dividing walls of hostility are being broken down by God's work. We are asked to look on the other side of those walls and find not the monsters we feared but the sisters and brothers for whom our hearts long. We are meant to live in community, and God is breaking down walls so that we can learn what it means to be human. The journey is perilous, but it offers hope and possibility. God is out ahead of us, leading us as God led the Israelites in the wilderness. It is a journey that God is calling us to make. Let us begin.

CHAPTER 2

"The Great Divide"*

It always has been the "great divide." From the beginning of the European history of this nation, it has defined us, directed us, and separated us. It is the power of the system of race, and its power continues unabated. We have come to a watershed on race relations in this society. We all had hoped that we had overcome, but we have not. Many of us are surprised and dismayed that we have returned to this great divide.

In the 1950s and 1960s, our nation experienced a tremendous human rights revolution, known as the civil rights movement, which focused on Americans of African descent, people who had been treated as slaves throughout most of the history of this country. For a brief time in our history, it appeared that it was possible to move closer to the great American vision that all people are created with equal dignity.

The gains of the civil rights movement were many and significant. Yet, some thirty years after the passage of the Voting Rights Act, we as a society find ourselves in a difficult position. Despite numerous important gains, more African-Americans live in poverty now than before the civil rights movement began. Despite gains in political power, many African-Americans, especially in urban areas, are locked into pockets of poverty,

---

* From Studs Terkel, *The Great Divide* (New York: Pantheon Books, 1988).

violence, and oppression. This never has been made more obvious than in the Rodney King case, which pulled the veneer off race relations in our time. The original verdict revealed a depth of racism that many whites thought had vanished forever. The rebellions in Los Angeles, Atlanta, and other cities in response to the verdict revealed a depth of African-American anger and bitterness that shocked white people.

The stories continue daily. Whether it is the growth in resegregation in the nation's schools (*Atlanta Constitution,* Dec. 14, 1993, A-1), the forced integration of an all-white housing project in Texas (*New York Times,* Jan. 14, 1994, A-1), or the growing white alarm over the continuing threat of violent crime (*Memphis Commercial Appeal,* Dec. 9. 1993, A-1), we clearly have failed to live out the vision of black and white together in this society.

As it always has, race remains central. It causes white parents to move their children from schools. It causes neighborhoods to change as whites flee from people of different colors who move into the neighborhoods. It causes people of darker color to refuse to share their lives with white people. We seem obsessed with race. Despite the civil rights movement, despite the rise of a black middle class, despite tremendous public achievement by people of darker color, race remains fundamental and central. One stunning example is a series of articles on race run over the course of six months (May-November 1993) by the New Orleans *Times-Picayune.* Entitled "Together Apart: The Myth of Race," it generated more than 7,000 phone calls from its readers. The cause of this stunning response was the series' premises that racial categories were not scientific and that racial barriers remained strong and powerful not only in New Orleans, but in the entire country. And New Orleans is known as a place of many mixed races! Yet, race still has its place.

The great divide of race remains with us. Even more disturbing is a growing difference concerning the reasons given for the persistence of race. As this chasm grows, we face a difficult situation. Many white people believe that we have done enough. Many white people believe that if black people continue to experience racial injustice or oppressive conditions, it is not the responsibility or fault of white people. We are witnessing a white denial of responsibility for the conditions of people of

darker color, especially those called black. Whites will acknowledge that poverty and lack of access to the mainstream are still
problems for black people. Yet, the reason given by many whites
for the problems of the African-American community is not
racism, but rather a deficit in African-Americans themselves,
whether an individual deficit or a collective deficit. Who is
responsible for the terrible condition of many black people in
this society? The answer given by most whites is "black people."
Thomas Edsall, in his book *Chain Reaction* (New York: W. W.
Norton, 1990), displays the prevailing white attitude when he
quotes Patrick Buchanan:

> Why did liberalism fail black America? Because it was built
> on a myth, the myth of the Kerner Commission, that the
> last great impediment to equality in America was "white
> racism." That myth was rooted in one of the oldest self-de-
> lusions: It is because you are rich that I am poor. My
> problems are your fault. You owe me! There was a time
> when white racism did indeed block black progress in
> America; but by the time of the Kerner Commission, ours
> was a nation committed to racial justice. The real root
> causes of the crisis in the underclass are twofold. First, the
> old character-forming, conscience-forming institutions,
> family, church, and school, have collapsed under relentless
> secular assault; second, as the internal constraints on be-
> havior were lost among the black poor, the external barri-
> ers—police, prosecutors, and courts—were systematically
> undermined…What the black poor need more than any-
> thing today is a dose of the truth. Slums are the products
> of the people who live there. Dignity and respect are not
> handed out like food stamps; they are earned and won.…
> The first step to progress, for any group, lies in the admis-
> sion that its failures are, by and large, its own fault, that
> success can come only through its own efforts, that, while
> the well-intentioned outsider may help, he or she is no
> substitute for personal sacrifice (p. 281).

On the other side are the African-American interpreters of the
current gap, who see the continuing emphasis on race and

continuing poverty and injustice as evidence of white recalcitrance. Indeed, Derrick Bell believes that white racism is a permanent part of American society because it "is a key component in this country's stability." In a foreboding comment in *Faces at the Bottom of the Well* (New York: Basic Books, 1992), Bell captures the feelings of most African-Americans.

> Consider: In this last decade of the twentieth century, color determines the social and economic status of all African Americans, both those who have been highly successful and their poverty-bound brethren whose lives are grounded in misery and despair. We rise and fall less as a result of our efforts than in response to the needs of a white society that condemns all blacks to quasi citizenship as surely as it segregated our parents and enslaved their forebears. The fact is that, despite what we designate as progress wrought through struggle over many generations, we remain what we were in the beginning: a dark and foreign presence, always the designated "other" (pp. x, 10).

Bell illuminates the central issue in the great divide. Racial categories were used to justify slavery, and those same categories continue to determine who will have access to power and who will not. Those of us who are white are incredulous when we hear words such as these. We cannot believe that racial categories remain so powerful. We are shocked to hear that black people are angry, frustrated, and bitter.

Some may wonder at this point why I seem to be taking a bi-polar approach to race, why I am focusing chiefly on "black" and "white." We are becoming multi-cultural in this country, and the pressures to address multi-cultural issues will continue to increase. I urge us not to move too quickly to multiculturalism without first working through the issues of black and white. In saying this, I am not denying massive discrimination and oppression and slaughter of Native Americans, Latino and Hispanic people, Asian, Mid-Eastern, Indian, and many other peoples who encounter this society. We must remember, however, that books like *The Bell Curve* emphasize black/white relations. While there is certainly a central connection between white attitudes toward all those classified as "non-white," the taproot of this racism lies in white attitudes toward those designated as "black." For white Americans, who hold the power to change, race begins and is centered on people called "black," and that obsession shall be this book's main focus.

Race is central to our identity as North Americans, as Andrew Hacker, Martin Luther King, Jr., Malcolm X, and many others have reminded us.* Race determines almost every door of opportunity in our lives. If we are the "right" race (white), many doors open up automatically without our ever noticing it. If we are the "wrong" race (black especially, but also Latino, Asian, and Native American), it is a struggle to open any door. While those who are white have officially proclaimed that race is no longer the watershed it once was, all who live in our society know that the truth is otherwise. Race is fundamental. Indeed, the importance of race is growing and beginning to reach depths that many of us felt would never be reached again.

Because the system of racial classification so favors those of us called white, we rarely understand the continuing depth of its power. We believed that by passing some laws, we could change hearts—it has not happened. I am not demeaning the passage of these laws. They are fundamental, and we need many more. The passage of laws and Supreme Court decisions related to the civil rights movement were not the ending of the matter, however; they were only the beginning. In many ways, we have stopped at the beginning, rather than going on. We who are white tend to think that the work is over, but it has only just begun. For those of us who want to believe that the power of the system of race has diminished, there is listening to be done, listening not only to the urban guerrillas but also to successful black people.

In his memoir, *Days of Grace* (New York: Knopf, 1993), written

---

* For a blunt treatment of the white view of race, see Andrew Hacker, *Two Nations* (New York: Charles Scribner & Sons, 1991). For an intriguing and helpful comparison of Malcolm X and Martin Luther King, Jr., see James Cone, *Martin and Malcolm and America* (Maryknoll, NY: Orbis Books, 1991).

before his death from complications of AIDS, tennis great Arthur Ashe shared a conversation he had with a magazine reporter in an interview about AIDS.

> "Mr. Ashe, I guess this must be the heaviest burden you have ever had to bear, isn't it?" she asked finally.
>
> I thought for a moment, but only a moment. "No, it isn't. It's a burden, all right. But AIDS isn't the heaviest burden I have had to bear."
>
> "Is there something worse? Your heart attack?"
>
> I didn't want to detain her, but I let the door close with both of us still inside. "You're not going to believe this," I said to her, "but being black is the greatest burden I've had to bear."
>
> "You can't mean that."
>
> "No question about it. Race has always been my biggest burden. Having to live as a minority in America. Even now it continues to feel like an extra weight tied around me."
>
> I can still recall the surprise and perhaps even the hurt on her face. I may even have surprised myself, because I simply had never thought of comparing the two conditions before. However, I stand by my remark. Race is for me a more onerous burden than AIDS. My disease is the result of biological factors over which we, thus far, have had no control. Racism, however, is entirely made by people, and therefore hurts and inconveniences infinitely more (pp. 126-27).

Ellis Close, in *The Rage of a Privileged Class* (New York: Harper Collins, 1993), cited the continuing anger and frustration of middle-class black people in relation to the system of race. The comments by Ashe, Close, and others strike white people as strange. Why are they complaining? They have been allowed to share in the economic pie of this society, and still they continue to complain about race. It is as if the status of being middle class should erase the problem of race, thus reducing race to a class problem. We forget that Ashe was not allowed to play tennis on the public courts in his hometown of Richmond, Virginia. How do you lose that memory? What do you do with it? We forget that on any given day Ashe would not be first and foremost a great tennis player. He would be first and foremost a black, perhaps a black person, but always a *black* person.

It is this lack of understanding that plagues people who call themselves white. Failure to feel guilt is not our problem. Many of us feel guilty about the historical treatment of people of darker color, especially those we call black. A much larger problem for us is denial, but not denial of the past. Rather, we deny the present: Race is still fundamental in our society. We believe that the power of race has been defeated, that the playing field has been leveled, and that the race of life can now be run. May the most competent person win!

Black people know otherwise. Whatever their economic status, they know that they are only a step away from a return to the overt oppression of their parents or grandparents, whether it is being pulled over and frisked by a police officer, being excluded from a particular club, or being seen as a monster when moving into a new neighborhood. White people seem unable and unwilling to acknowledge that this thing called "the burden of race" still remains strong.

Because of the continuing power of racial classification and the denial of its continuing power by white people, we must take some time to explore the origins of the system. A full treatment is beyond the scope of this book, but we must visit it briefly to understand its continuing power. We may find that we are much more like our parents than we may want to imagine.

To discern the source of the enduring power of racial classification, we must return to its terms and the origins of the system itself. The first thing to notice about the system of race is its primary colors: white and black. There is initial puzzlement about these primary colors, for they do not describe actual skin colors. There are many different skin colors—peach, tan, brown, beige, olive, chocolate, and so on—but no one is actually black or white. The primary colors of the system of race are not descriptive; they are intentionally exaggerated.

Despite the arbitrary nature of the primary colors of the system of race, our classification according to this system is fundamental. Race is the most important classification one has in this society. Although class and gender rival it, race is of fundamental importance. This characteristic of the system of race and its arbitrary nature make it striking and troubling.

The idea of race began in the colonial period of European history; it was first used in 1684 by a French scientist (Jacques Barzun, *Race: A Study in Superstition* [New York: Harper & Row, 1965], p. 35). The idea of race was accepted as scientific fact during this period. The distinguished Swedish scientist Carolus Linneaus classified four races of human beings in 1738:

> *Homo Americanus*—Tenacious, contented, free; ruled by custom.
> *Homo Eurpoaeus*—Light, lively, inventive; ruled by rites.
> *Homo Asiaticus*—Stern, haughty, stingy; ruled by opinion.
> *Homo Afer*—Cunning, slow, negligent; ruled by caprice (Barzun, p. 45).

This list reveals the motivation behind the development of the idea of racial classification. It became a powerful ideological tool in the process of conquering and colonizing the world. Europeans are "light, lively and inventive," while Africans are "cunning, slow, and negligent." Whatever the origin of the idea of race, the scientific community has now abandoned it. Joanna L. Mountain, a Stanford University geneticist, puts it this way: "The differences between people may be visible, but the labels we impose on them biologically don't make any sense. Culturally and socially, it's very much a reality. Biologically, it's just not meaningful. We're a big messy soup of people."[*]

The difficult truth is that racial classification is not a scientific category or biological classification. It is a social and political construct designed to determine who should have access to power and who should not. Racial classification is not an objec-

---

[*] "Racism Spawned by Unscientific Data and Europeans' Need to Feel Superior," James O'Bryne, *The Atlanta Constitution*, Dec. 26, 1993, p. M-4. For more in-depth treatment, see Theodore Allen, *The Invention of the White Race* (New York: Verso, 1994); Ashley Montagu, *Man's Most Dangerous Myth: The Fallacy of Race* (Cambridge: Oxford University Press, 1974); Thomas Gossett, *Race: The History of an Idea in America* (New York: Schocken Books, 1963).

tive category discovered by the scientific method. It is a system whose purpose is to indicate who has control and who is controlled. This system of race, haphazardly constructed but powerful nonetheless, lifts up the humanity and the abilities of one group of people—those called white. It seeks to deny the humanity and belittle the abilities of all those classified as nonwhite or colored. This is the taproot of the enduring power of racism.

In a scientific sense, there are no white people in our society—there are no black people. There are many different skin colors, facial features, and hair types. There is a rainbow of humanity. Rather than celebrate this diversity, however, we have chosen to turn it into an ugly monster.

The system of race not only denies the humanity of people of darker color. It also works to assign responsibility for this racism not to the whites, who created the system, but to the people of darker color, who suffer from it. People of darker color are forced into the position of having to prove themselves to white people: If there is injustice, if there is racism, it is said to be because darker people and darker cultures are inferior. This is at the heart of the system of race. White people are good and in control. Darker people are bad (or inadequate) and should be controlled. If there is inequity, it is because of the innate differences in the races. As Linneaus put it so "scientifically," Europeans are light and lively, while Africans are slow and negligent, and Asians are stingy and ruled by opinion.

This brings us back to the great divide. White people believe that the power of race is over—darker people experience racial classification as central. The dialogue between these two positions will, to a large extent, determine the course of this country in the next century. For us to to be able to ensure that the dialogue will be helpful and not damaging, we must first understand how the system of race continues to work; then we must seek to change its power over us. The remainder of this book is an attempt to help us take those two essential steps: understanding and changing. If we cannot take these steps, we will doom our society to continuing to see diversity in skin color as a source of tremendous problems. If we can take these steps, however, we will help our society make great progress toward affirming the vision that is great within us: the equal dignity of all human beings.

CHAPTER 3

"I Have a Dream Today"

After a great civil rights movement, we find ourselves as a society asking what went wrong. We thought that we had corrected the oppression of black people through the civil rights movement, but the great divide remains, and the oppressive conditions seem more intractable than ever. It is a disheartening time, but it is not the first time we have faced this dilemma.

Following the Civil War, a grand experiment in democracy was tried. It was an attempt to put into institutional flesh the powerful words of the Declaration of Independence: "We hold these truths to be self-evident—that all men are created equal." The period known as Reconstruction was a time when we as a people barely dipped our toes into the waters of equality. It lasted only ten years, and it failed because white people did not want equality. We did not want to share power with black people. The sad story is a saga for another book, but we have passed this way one hundred years ago.*

---

* For a history of Reconstruction and its aftermath, see Lerone Bennett, *Black Power USA: The Human Side of Reconstruction, 1867-1877* (New York: Penguin Books, 1967); W. E. B. DuBois, *Black Reconstruction in America, 1860-1880* (New York: Atheneum, 1962); Richard Kluger, *Simple Justice* (New York: Random House Vintage Books, 1975); Eric Foner, *Reconstruction—America's Unfinished Revolution, 1863-1877* (New York: Harper & Row, 1988); John Hope Franklin, *Reconstruction After the Civil War* (Chicago: University of Chicago Press, 1961).

"I have a dream today." No other speech in our time so captured the hopes of the modern human rights movement as well as Martin Luther King, Jr.'s, speech given in the sweltering August heat in Washington in 1963. Almost as if passing the torch of the movement's leadership, W. E. B. DuBois died in Ghana on the same day King gave this speech. After decades of oppression, with lonely voices such as DuBois and Ida B. Wells, who led the antilynching movement in the 1890s, and Thurgood Marshall speaking for freedom, the voice of hope and justice was heard once again in the land.

> So I say to you my friends, that even though we must face the difficulties of today and tomorrow, I still have a dream. It is a dream deeply rooted in the American dream that one day this nation will rise up and live out the true meaning of its creed—we hold these truths to be self-evident, that all men are created equal.
>
> I have a dream that one day on the red hills of Georgia, sons of former slaves and sons of former slave owners will be able to sit down together at the table of brotherhood.
>
> I have a dream that one day, even the state of Mississippi, a state sweltering with the heat of injustice, sweltering with the heat of oppression, will be transformed into an oasis of freedom and justice.
>
> I have a dream that my four little children will one day live in a nation where they will not be judged by the color of their skin but by the content of their character. I have a dream today!

King spoke of the hopes and motivations that led us as a nation through a second experiment in democracy. Although there are no precise dates for the beginning of the second experiment, most observers date it from two events. The first was the May 17, 1954, *Brown v. Board of Education* unanimous Supreme Court decision, which overturned the May 18, 1896, *Plessy v. Ferguson* decision. In the *Brown* case, the Court threw out "separate but equal" with regard to public schools. The second event was Rosa Parks's refusal to give up her seat in the white section of the bus in Montgomery on December 1, 1955, which recalled the spirit and resistance of Ida B. Wells when she refused to give up her seat on a train in Tennessee in 1884.* With these events, the struggle for racial justice seemed to catch fire, and the need for steps toward justice moved closer to the forefront of public awareness. Although there was no massive and destructive war in the modern movement, as there had been in the last century with the Civil War, there was a war of words, ideas, and wills; and there was violence and death.

By the time of the Washington march in 1963, at which King gave his famous speech, there had already been startling change. The buses in Montgomery had been boycotted and finally ordered desegregated; federal troops had enforced the Supreme Court order to integrate schools in Little Rock; black students all over the South had "sat in" at lunch counters previously reserved for whites; freedom riders had integrated public transportation in the South and been beaten for it; James Meredith had become the first black student to enroll at the University of Mississippi (with a white riot to follow); and police dogs had been turned loose on black children in Birmingham. Much more would happen after this gathering in Washington. President John F. Kennedy would be assassinated; students and others would lead a massive voter registration campaign in Mississippi Freedom Summer; the Civil Rights Act would pass in 1964; and the Voting Rights Act would pass in 1965—followed ten days later by a widespread rebellion by black people in the Watts section of Los Angeles.

Even in the face of all the reactionary violence and white resistance, the progress was considerable. President Lyndon B. Johnson, rather than saying that he was tired of the Negro, as President Grant had said ninety years earlier, joined in the push for democracy and equal rights. President Johnson said: "We shall overcome," in a nationally televised speech to a joint session of Congress in 1965 after the white violence at Selma, Alabama.

---

* The story of Ida B. Wells is told in Ida B. Wells, *Crusade for Justice, The Autobiography of Ida B. Wells*, ed. Alfreda M. Duster (Chicago: The University of Chicago Press, 1970), pp. 18-20.

Indeed, much was done to promote human rights for all. This echo of Reconstruction promised the possibility that the ideal of all people being created with equal dignity would become truth in the United States. The Thirteenth, Fourteenth, and Fifteenth Amendments began to be reaffirmed; and the Supreme Court seemed inclined to uphold them rather than strip them of their meaning and authority. This was a time of great opportunity and some progress. The War on Poverty was born, the seeds of affirmative action were sown, and the dignity and humanity of African-American people were beginning to be affirmed. The years 1964 to 1968 seemed to promise great possibilities, and the system of race seemed to be faltering with the passage of the Civil Rights Act and the Voting Rights Act.

As with Reconstruction, however, there were disturbing voices. White violence rang out—President Kennedy was assassinated, civil rights workers were beaten and murdered, and citizens were killed as they endeavored to exercise their constitutional rights. In a sad commentary on King's stirring speech in Washington, whites waited only eighteen days before bombing Sixteenth Street Baptist Church in Birmingham on a bloody Sunday, killing four black girls. African-Americans had learned from history also. This time they would not be as cooperative with the white agenda as whites thought they ought to be. In the summer of 1965, black rebellions broke out in Harlem, Watts, Detroit, and many other places. A prophet born in Nebraska and reared in the training grounds of Northern ghettos and prisons indicated that the power of racism was much deeper than anyone wanted to admit. Malcolm X answered King's dream with the nightmare:

> Unemployment and poverty have forced many of our people into this life of crime; but...the real criminal is in City Hall downtown. The real criminal is in the State House in Albany. The real criminal is in the White House in Washington, D.C. The real criminal is the white man who poses as a liberal—the political hypocrite. And it is these legal crooks, posing as our friends, [who are] forcing us into a life of crime and then using us to spread the white man's evil vices among our own people. Our people are

scientifically maneuvered by the white man into a life of poverty. You are not poor accidentally. He maneuvers you into poverty. You are not a drug addict accidentally. Why, the white man maneuvers you into drug addiction. You are not a prostitute accidentally. You have been maneuvered into prostitution by the American white man. There is nothing about your condition here in America that is an accident.*

The idea of black power took hold. African-American people began to assert their own agenda, and it deeply disturbed white people who thought they knew best for black people. The tensions grew as white people saw that black people really intended to have power and access. As the tensions grew, the dream and the nightmare would converge in the usual way in the system of race—both King and Malcolm X would be victims of its violence.

By 1966, the tide had begun to turn. In that year, the Republicans gained forty-seven seats in the U.S. House of Representatives. The political party that had tied itself to Goldwater in 1964 and had supposedly been crushed now began to make its comeback, building on the politics of race.** Also in 1966, Ronald Reagan was elected governor of California on the strength of the white suburban vote. From here, he built the base that enabled him to lead the white movement as president. Building on the voting shifts in 1966, the year 1968 was pivotal in the entrenchment of white society to resist the gains of the civil rights movement. After eight years of Democratic support for the civil rights movement (albeit reluctant support at times), the Republicans won the presidency on the strength of the white reaction to the civil rights movement. Four factors influenced

---

* James H. Cone, *Martin and Malcolm and America: A Dream or Nightmare?* (Maryknoll, NY: Orbis Books, 1991), p. 89.

** Edsall has an excellent analysis of how the Republican party regained its political power by building on race in *Chain Reaction* (New York: W. W. Norton, 1990).

this election: the conflicts that revolved around the Vietnam War, the decision of President Lyndon Johnson not to seek a second term, the first redemption of Richard Nixon, and the emergence of George Wallace as a presidential contender and voice for whites who did not want to share power with black people. In the 1968 vote, whites showed their preference and their power— Nixon and Wallace had a combined 57 percent of the vote.

To my point of view, Wallace was the most important factor, because he sought to legitimize the power of racism by asserting that the civil rights movement of the 1950s and 1960s had discriminated against white people. Called reverse discrimination, this claim later became the hallmark of the white movement to refuse access to black people. Wallace shifted the ground of resistance to the gains of the civil rights movement. Instead of shouting "White Power!" he shouted "Discrimination!" and thus the debate centered not on white resistance but on the deprivation of rights for white people. The most important contribution by Wallace was to enable whites to make their case for keeping power without ever referring to racism.*

Just as whites had tired of black struggles for justice during Reconstruction, so did they in 1968. Norman Mailer, who covered both political conventions in 1968, wrote a book based on his experience. In *Miami and the Siege of Chicago* (New York: The World Publishing Co., 1968) he offered this confession on behalf of many white people on the occasion of Ralph Abernathy's late appearance for a meeting at the Republican convention:

> Still it was unduly irritating to have to wait at a press conference, and as the minutes went by and annoyance mounted, the reporter became aware after a while of a curious emotion in himself, for he had not ever felt it consciously before—it was a simple emotion and very unpleasant to him—he was getting tired of Negroes and their rights....What an obsession was the Negro to the

---

* For an intriguing discussion of Wallace as part of the Populist tradition, see Stephan Lesher, *George Wallace: American Populist* (Reading, MA: Addison-Wesley, 1994).

average white American by now. Every time that American turned in his thoughts to the sweetest object of con-
templation in his mind's small town bower, nothing less
than America the Beautiful herself—the angel of security
at the end of every alley—then there was the face of an
accusing rioting Black right in the middle of the dream—
smack in the center of the alley (p. 51).

In only four short years, beginning with the passage of the
Civil Rights Act in 1964, the second civil rights movement had
blossomed, borne promising fruit, and begun to be rejected by
white society.

During the years since 1968, there has been a resurgence of
white power over black people, a return to the system of race as
fundamental, and an attempt to disavow the gains of this second
human rights movement. There has been less overt violence in
this modern repudiation; more often it has taken a more subtle
but still deadly course—the gradual and systematic stripping of
the humanity of black people. As James Cone put it in *Martin
and Malcolm and America*, the dream of the second human rights
movement would soon become a nightmare.

During the years that followed the first human rights movement, white people stymied the gains of Reconstruction by
returning to race. In the conflict between equality and race,
whites chose race. In this choice, whites reasserted race as fundamental and sought to strip black people of their humanity to
blunt the power of the idea of equality. They did this by violence,
by discrediting the human rights movement, and by blaming
black people for its failure. In the modern era, white people are
using the same methods in their struggle to re-establish the
primacy of race and racism. Although there is not as much white
violence as there was one hundred years ago, white violence still
breaks out, from the reemergence of the Ku Klux Klan, to Con-
intelpro (the FBI attack on King, the Black Panthers, and others),
to the current occupying armies of the ghettos known as the
police (ask Rodney King or Malice Green), to Bensonhurst, to
Howard Beach, to Bernhard Goetz. This is not to suggest that
the police understand their purpose to be that of an occupying
army whose duty it is to repress black people, but rather that

many black people see the police in that manner. It also raises the vital issue of the tension between *intent* and *results.*

Racial discrimination has always worked best when intent is emphasized over results. Those who benefit from the system of race gain the most when the intent to discriminate is disavowed. The U.S. Supreme Court endorsed this idea in the 1890s when it upheld the new constitutions of southern states, which resulted in disenfranchising black voters. Despite clear demonstrations that these constitutions would result in denying the vote to black people, the Supreme Court upheld them because they expressed no intent to disenfranchise. Thus, in our time, the intent of the police may not be to extend the forces of racism or to serve as an occupying army. It may be to deter crime. Yet, this lack of conscious intent cannot invalidate the results when the police act as a force of racism or when they are seen by many in the African-American community as an occupying army.

This tension between intent and results is essential in understanding the resurgence of racism in our time. I am not suggesting that there is a massive, conscious conspiracy to disempower people of darker color, although there are conscious political strategies to win votes based on race. We will visit these strategies shortly. I am suggesting, however, that the drama of a return to racism is being seen again in our time. From a white point of view, there is no racism if there is no intent to judge by race. From a black point of view, the expressed intent is relatively unimportant in comparison with the results of the actions of white people.

Racial discrimination functions best when intent is emphasized over results. Most white people will not publicly claim any intent to discriminate based on race. Many white people may not be aware of any conscious attempt on their part to judge by race. For those of us who claim the name white, this lack of conscious intent to discriminate means we are not racist and we do not participate in the system of race. However, the results of our actions indicate otherwise when we flee neighborhoods into which black people move because we are afraid our property values will drop. When a white banker "red-lines" a neighborhood, the rationale is not that people of darker color live there but that the neighborhood contains bad credit risks. When a school system places a vastly disproportionate number of black children in special education classes, it is not because of their racial classification but because of their low socioeconomic level. White people use these rationales externally and internally to avoid acknowledging the continuing power of race in our lives.

When I assert that race has been reestablished primarily in response to the civil rights movement, I am not asserting a vast conspiracy. I am asserting that the fundamental power of race is so great that it operates regardless of the level of consciousness. In other words, the humanity and equality of African-Americans are not currently in dispute in public discourse. Even David Duke felt compelled to use code language for race and to deny his Klan heritage in his political campaigns. Yet we must not deceive ourselves in this crucial period. The system of race is making a strong comeback in response to the idea of the equality of black people. This growing racism is developing despite white disavowals of it. It is developing because in our culture the idea of race is stronger than the idea of equality.

Part of the reason for this growth of racism is that white people still feel threatened by people of darker color, especially African-American people. This sense of fear on the part of white people at the destruction of the system of race (and its accompanying racism) is no exaggeration. It is essential to acknowledge how deep and painful this threat is to white people. Thomas Edsall reports one clear example of this fear in a 1985 study conducted by Stanley Greenberg, now a political consultant to President Bill Clinton. The 1985 study was conducted in Macomb County, a white working-class suburb on the edge of Detroit. The Democrats studied it because of the county's dramatic shift in presidential voting. In 1960, this district went 63 percent to 37 percent Democratic for Kennedy over Nixon. In 1984, it went 63 percent to 33 percent Republican for Reagan over Mondale. What happened to cause the shift? Greenberg's summary tells us:

> These white Democratic defectors express a profound distaste for blacks, a sentiment that pervades almost everything they think about government and politics....Blacks constitute the explanation for their [white defectors'] vul-

nerability and for almost everything that has gone wrong in their lives; not being black is what constitutes being middle class; not living with blacks is what makes a neighborhood a decent place to live. These sentiments have important implications for Democrats, as virtually all progressive symbols and themes have been redefined in racial and pejorative terms....The special status of blacks is perceived by almost all of these individuals as a serious obstacle to their personal advancement. Indeed, discrimination against whites has become a well-assimilated and ready explanation for their status, vulnerability and failures....Ronald Reagan's image [was] formed against this [Democratic] backdrop—disorder and weakness, passivity, and humiliation and a party that failed to speak for the average person. By contrast, Reagan represented a determined consistency and an aspiration to unity and pride (Edsall, p. 182).

Although the Republican party has benefited the most from this reaction, it did not cause it. The reaction was there, waiting to be tapped politically. The Democratic party is now playing to this same reaction, as it distances itself from black leaders such as Jesse Jackson and takes up the banner with code words for race such as *welfare* and *crime.*

It is worth a brief examination of this process to learn how it has worked in seeking to reverse the gains of the second civil rights movement. The first step in this process was to aggravate the nerve that George Wallace had touched with his emphasis on reverse discrimination. This step argued that in seeking to repair the damage that black people had suffered from the injustice of the past, white people in the present were themselves being denied equal justice.

The next step was to talk about government intrusion in the lives of white individuals and white people as a group. Just as the Northern federal government had intruded in the lives of white Southerners during Reconstruction, it is asserted, so now that same federal government is intruding in the lives of all white people. In this sense, white people who would seem to have little in common are united in a major area. They believe that they suffer from reverse discrimination resulting from excessive governmental zeal in seeking to redress previous wrongs against black people. A white Southerner and a white union member near Detroit are thus held together by the system of race, without using overtly racist language.

The third step in this process, closely related to the second, has been to drop the vocabulary of race from the public debate. Indeed, this move enabled the Republicans to win votes of white Democrats who had previously supported Kennedy and Johnson. This deletion of the language of race has been a major step in the shift, as Edsall indicates:

> The importance of excising the language of race from American right-wing politics—a politics long burdened with a history of explicit racism and a politics that had often had, particularly in the South, a race-conscious intent—cannot be overestimated. In facing an electorate with sharply divided commitments on race—theoretically in favor of egalitarian principle but hostile to many forms of implementation—the use of a race-free political language proved crucial to building a broad-based, center-right coalition (p. 138).

The deletion of overt racism has been an important step, because it has enabled society to return to an emphasis on intent rather than results. If race language is taken out of public debate, then the charge of racism can be refuted, because no racist intent has been expressed. In this scenario, if the results of society's actions seem racist, it is not because white society intended to be racist. White people can then affirm that it is not racism that is hurting African-American people. It may be the huge federal deficit that is hurting them, or it may be a deficit in African-American people themselves, but it is not racism that is afflicting them. Thus, in a macabre development, whites and blacks can agree that blacks are afflicted abnormally in this society, but disagree whether racism is responsible for the affliction.

This assertion of intent over results in regard to racism can be used in many ways. For instance, in any debate over attempts to reduce the federal deficit, the proposed cuts in social programs often adversely affect African-American people. When some object to the cuts because they seem racially motivated, the answer given is that the cuts are not aimed at African-Americans or any other people of color. The response is that the federal deficit must be trimmed and taxes must be decreased. It can then be affirmed by most whites that it is not racism that is hurting African-Americans. This line of reasoning claims that African-American people have become too dependent on government spending "giveaways," and if they have indeed been hurt by decreased government spending, that has been a harsh but necessary price to be paid in cutbacks in government spending. It is the power of race in action without ever having to claim it. And there can be no doubt that this process continues today. The state of California had on its November 1992 ballot an initiative called *The Taxpayer Protection Act* "that would, among other things, cut welfare benefits by ten percent, along with an additional fifteen percent for families with an able-bodied adult that have been on the rolls for six months."

A Times Mirror Center poll released on September 20, 1994, indicated these dramatic shifts in this area (*Atlanta Constitution,* Sept. 21, 1994, p. A-1). In 1987, 71 percent of those polled felt that the government should take care of those who couldn't care for themselves. In 1994, that percentage had fallen to 57 percent. In 1987, 46 percent agreed that equal rights for minorities had been pushed too far. In 1994, agreement with the idea of overreaching had risen to a majority of 51 percent.

A new language has emerged, enabling white society to attack African-American people without resorting to traditional racist language. Using Wallace's emphasis on reverse discrimination was a start, but it referred only to white people. There was a need for an approach that referred to black people, a language that once again shifted the responsibility for the repudiation of human rights from white people to black people. Rather than understanding that racism is the central cause of the continuing distress of many African-Americans, whites have redeveloped the 100-year-old post-Reconstruction approach that asserts that the continued oppression and poverty of African-Americans are their responsibilities, not the responsibilities of whites. The terms used to describe black distress speak of a "culture of poverty," "culturally deprived," "behaviorally dependent," "black underclass." All of these terms imply a deficit in African-American people, a lack that is to be traced to them rather than to the system in which they have been placed.

Over the past decade, we have seen articles and conferences on "What's wrong with the black family?" and "What's wrong with black men?" For example, the cover of *Newsweek* of August 30, 1993, has a picture of a young black boy with the title: "A World Without Fathers: The Struggle to Save the Black Family." It is rare to see an article or conference entitled "What's Wrong With the White Family?" Rather than deal with the forces causing the collapse of all families, the media have chosen to isolate the black family. Any analysis of the black experience that begins without first grounding it in the system of race fails to grasp the dynamics of the situation. Yet, again and again, we see this process because we as a society are returning to a denial of the humanity and equality of people of darker color, especially those called black. This kind of analysis allowed the Bush administration to blame the violence in Los Angeles on welfare programs instead of on the system of race. It should be no surprise, then, that "welfare," "family values," and "crime" became central issues in the 1992 and 1994 elections. They are the "Willie Hortons" of this political season.

In light of this, the disturbing results of the 1994 Congressional elections should not be as shocking as they first appeared. As we will see later, almost every major campaign issue that appealed to voters in the 1994 elections had "race" at its root: welfare, family values, crime, education. The furor over orphanages as an alternative to welfare is not about saving money. It costs $36,000 a year to keep a boy in Newt Gingrich's beloved Boys' Town, a cost light years above the average welfare cost. The 1994 fall elections were the voice of white people seeking to take back a country that we feel that we have lost. Almost 66 percent of white men who went to the poles voted Republican, and 55 percent of white women did the same.*

---

*"More men casting lot with GOP," (*Atlanta Constitution,* November 11, 1994, p. A-9).

Masking the system of race by using code language is essential to continuing white control. What has captured public debate, even after the Rodney King verdict, is not the continuing racism of white people, but what Thomas Edsall calls the war between "taxpayers" and "tax recipients" (p. 29). Rather than saying whites versus people of darker color, we say taxpayers versus tax recipients. The taxpayers (white) are those who work hard, pay taxes, and thus support the society. The tax recipients ("colored") do not work, receive tax payments, and are a drain on society. The importance of this code language was seen in reactions to President Bush's broken promise of "Read my lips— no new taxes," made at the Republican convention of 1988. When he made that remarkable promise in light of the huge federal deficit, he touched the longing of people to get government off their backs. He also touched on the primary reason, as white people saw it, that government was on their backs—to correct the ills of the system of race. In pledging no new taxes, Bush signaled to white people that government "intrusion" into their lives would be stopped.

Nowadays, this idea of big government intrusion into our lives seems rooted in race. While we as white people have taken only baby steps in seeking to overcome race, it feels like we have been forced to take huge, giant steps. And, who forced us to do it? The federal government, of course! So, if we can downsize the federal government, we won't have anyone big enough to force us to deal with race.

This attitude of taxpayers vs. tax recipients is not just for "white" people. Middle-class people of all colors have accepted this interpretation without adequately understanding its basis. Thus, many black, Latino, and Asian middle-class folk respond positively to this interpretation and see the "non-white" poor as the enemy and as the cause of their continuing problems.

Taxpayers versus tax recipients—it is one of the codes for race in our time. It speaks of government intrusion in our lives, forcing us who are white to live, go to school, and work with those we would rather avoid—people of darker color. While it is a strong motivation of current public policy, its lack of reality should be obvious. All of us are tax recipients in some way. We all receive government benefits, whether it is a standing army, road repair, social security, or police and fire protection.

William Schneider also spoke to this phenomenon in an important article in *The Atlantic* (July 1992, pp. 33-44). He indicated that the 1992 presidential election was the first in our history in which a majority of the voters was suburban. The suburbs have grown because of white flight from the cities as white people seek safety and security among their own kind. As black politicians are elected in the cities, white people move out to recover ownership of government.

> A major reason people move out to the suburbs is simply to be able to buy their own government. These people resent it when politicians take their money and use it to solve other people's problems, especially when they don't believe that government can actually solve those problems (p. 37).

Flight from the cities is a flight from people of darker color, especially from black people. Although flight by white people is the most important dynamic, black people are also fleeing the city. While black flight is complex, at its heart, it seems to be an acceptance of the view of the system of race: where there are black people, there is crime and violence and decadence. Thus, flight to the suburbs is not only a phenomenon of white people—black people and other darker peoples are also fleeing. Having said this, however, it must be clear—compared to white flight, black flight is miniscule. And, for black people, class status of the neighbors is the most important factor in the decision to move. For white people, class status is relatively unimportant: racial classification is the central factor in the decision to move.

This is a brief summary of the process by which public discourse has changed in regard to politics and race. It was initiated by the Republican party, but both major political parties have now accepted this approach and use it. This is one major example of how the gains of the civil rights movement are being reversed. The first verdict in the Rodney King case tells us how white people in the suburbs view a black man surrounded by police—not as a citizen about to be assaulted by government forces, but a dangerous animal who must be brought under control by any means necessary. Rather than being an aberration as many had hoped, the verdict accurately reflects where we are as a society.

Just as the Supreme Court decisions were essential in dismantling the human rights gains of Reconstruction, so its decisions are central today. Over the past fifteen years, the Court has joined its predecessor of one hundred years ago in seeking to dismantle the gains of the civil rights movement. As was the case then, the Supreme Court has used "intentionality" as a key concept. If *intent* to discriminate by skin color cannot be proven, then there is no constitutional redress for any resulting discrimination. In other words, no matter how much discrimination is demonstrated as factual, no matter how much it is shown that the system of race favors white people over ethnic people of darker color, there is no constitutional violation unless *intent* to favor white people or otherwise discriminate is shown. No matter what the results, if no intent can be proven, there is no violation of the Constitution.

The Alan Bakke case came to the Court in 1978 after a white man challenged the University of California's medical school admission policies. Bakke claimed that he had been denied admission because there were slots set aside for people of darker color and, although he did not use the words "reverse discrimination," he claimed that he had been discriminated against because he was white. The Court upheld the admissions policy but ordered Bakke to be admitted to medical school. It was a small but significant first crack in the wall of affirmative action.

A much larger crack came in 1989. The Court had previously ruled, in *Griggs v. Duke Power* (1971), that discrimination in employment policies was just that, whether or not it could be proved that such discrimination was intentional. In that case, the *results* were more important than the intent. It was a victory for equal rights that recognized the depth and power of the system of race. In 1989, however, the Court took a giant step away from that victory in *Wards Cove Packing v. Antonio.* In this case, the burden of proof was shifted from the employer (results) to the employee (intent). Now the Court ruled the employee must not only demonstrate that there is discrimination as a result of policies but also that there was *intent* to discriminate.

Two other 1989 cases have to do with the idea of reverse discrimination. In *City of Richmond v. J. A. Croson Co.*, the Court ruled in favor of a white plaintiff who claimed that Richmond's "set aside" program was unconstitutional. The city of Richmond, Virginia, like many other cities, had routinely set aside contracts for minority employers. The Supreme Court ruled that this policy unfairly discriminated against whites. An even stronger blow at affirmative action came in *Martin v. Wicks*. This decision permitted white firefighters in Birmingham, Alabama, to challenge a consent decree that lifted up affirmative action for black firefighters. The most important part here is that the Supreme Court's action overturned a court-validated consent decree signed by all parties in 1979. Thus, the Court ordered a lower federal court to reopen a ten-year-old case that had been settled.

The Supreme Court further eroded its (and our) commitment to equal rights in three other 1992 decisions. In January by a 6-3 vote in *Presley v. Etowah County*, the Court limited the scope of the 1965 Voting Rights Act by ruling that counties in Alabama could arbitrarily change the duties of county commissioners after black county commissioners were elected for the first time. In this case, the majority white county commissioners took duties previously held by individual county commissioners and placed them under the entire commission. Prior to the election of black commissioners, each commissioner had discretionary powers over roadworks in their individual districts. That policy was changed so that the black commissioners would have no discretionary power. In March 1992, the Court voted 8-0 (Thurgood Marshall had retired) in a Dekalb County, Georgia, desegregation case to make it much easier for school districts to be released from federal court jurisdiction, even if those districts remained unintentionally segregated.* In this case, Dekalb County's school board admitted that some of its schools re-

---

* These two rulings of the Supreme Court were reported, respectively, in the *New York Times*, Jan. 27, 1992, p. A-1 and the *Atlanta Constitution*, April 1, 1992, p. A-1.

mained segregated. The board argued, however, that the schools were the result of housing patterns and not intentional segregation by the school system. The Supreme Court upheld this argument, and the emphasis was on intent and not results.

The third case is perhaps the most poignant. In April 1992, the Court set aside a lower court ruling in a Topeka, Kansas, school desegregation suit. The Supreme Court ordered the lower court to reconsider its ruling that the Topeka school board had not done enough to promote racial balance. This is the same district that served as the lead case in the historic *Brown v. Board of Education* ruling in 1954. The case began again in 1979, when the parents of seventeen black Topeka students brought the suit against the Topeka school board. In an ironic but not surprising note, one of the parents who initiated the suit was Linda Brown, who had been an elementary school student in Topeka in 1954. Her name was used in the historic *Brown* case. She has watched the Supreme Court make a significant and distressing departure from a commitment to equality in the 38 years since *Brown v. Board of Education*. The case is currently in the lower court.

In a redistricting mandated by the 1990 census, some states, including Georgia and North Carolina, sought to create congressional districts that would give African-American and Hispanic candidates a better chance to win. In the summer of 1993, in response to a suit brought by white voters, the Supreme Court threw out one such district in North Carolina by a 5-4 vote. The Court based its decision on the position that any redistricting based on the racial classification of the members of the district "bears an uncomfortable resemblance to political apartheid." The Court seemed to ignore all other redistricting that seeks to strengthen white voting districts. It is interesting to note that the Court's decision came after more people of darker color were elected to Congress in 1992 than at any time since Reconstruction. In September 1994, a special three-judge federal panel rejected the boundaries of Georgia's 11th District, which had elected Georgia's first black congresswoman. As one attorney put it, if this court trend holds, "it will absolutely be *Plessy v. Ferguson* all over again" (*Atlanta Constitution,* Sept. 13, 1994, pp. A-1, E-4).

Perhaps nowhere is the Court's determination to keep the

system of race intact seen more clearly than in its attitude toward the use of the death penalty. The death penalty rarely has been used only as a response to murder. If it were, we would have many more executions. The death penalty has been used as a weapon of political control to maintain the systems of race and class. This is not to say that those who are executed are innocent. Though more innocent people have been executed than we can allow ourselves to admit, innocence is not the issue here. The issue is the use of the death penalty—who is charged with a capital offense, who is convicted, and who is executed. Black man after black man is given the death penalty for killing a stranger in a robbery. The use of the death penalty has been overwhelmingly applied to the poor, especially to African-Americans, regardless of class status. This is the only nation in the Western world that continues to use the death penalty, and its use is directly connected to the system of race.

The Supreme Court recognized the great disparity in the use of the death penalty in its 1972 decision in *Furman v. Georgia*. In that decision, it ruled by a 5-4 vote that the death penalty as applied at that time was unconstitutional because it was used in a cruel and unusual way (as reported by the Bureau of Justice Statistics Bulletin, July 1981). The Court did, however, invite the states to devise laws that sought a more equitable distribution of the death penalty. Some 35 states responded; in 1976, the Court upheld the death penalty statutes of Georgia, Florida, and Texas. The Court seemed undisturbed that of the 588 people on death row at that time, more than half were black people. This was vastly out of proportion to the general population (51 percent on death row compared with 12 percent of the population). It recognized that the death penalty has often been used as a weapon of terror in the system of race when it ruled in 1977, in *Coker v. Georgia*, that the rape of a female adult was not a capital offense. Applying the death penalty to this category had been reserved almost exclusively for black men. Since the Bureau of Justice began to keep statistics in 1930, more than 90 percent of all people executed for rape have been African-American men.

The Supreme Court's hope for an equitable distribution of the death penalty has not been met. Once again, the death penalty became a weapon for the maintenance of the system of race. One of the most compelling cases supporting this reality came in 1987 with *McCleskey v. Georgia*. By a 5-4 vote, the Court rejected a racial bias study by David Baldus of the University of Iowa which indicated that in the state of Georgia, people charged with killing white people were ten times more likely to receive the death penalty than those charged with killing black people. Those voting in the majority in this case chose to dismiss this startling evidence of racial bias in the application of the death penalty. The life of a white person was seen as worth much more than the life of a black person.

Justice Lewis Powell, who wrote for the majority, agreed that the study indicated racial bias. Yet he also claimed that race was so much a part of the system that it could not be overcome: "Apparent disparities in sentencing are an inevitable part of our criminal justice system" (*Atlanta Constitution,* April 22, 1987, p. A-1). Powell indicated that despite results that demonstrated racial bias, intent to establish that bias had not been proven. "Where the discretion that is fundamental to our criminal process is involved, we decline to assume that what is unexplained is invidious." Powell and his colleagues chose not to see the system of race as the explanation, because to do so would require a major overhaul of the judicial machine. Powell correctly perceived the threat posed by the McCleskey case: "McCleskey's claim, taken to its logical conclusion, throws into serious question the principles that underlie our entire criminal justice system" (*Atlanta Constitution,* p. A-1). (See the next chapter for an explanation of those principles.) The Court chose to step away from a confrontation with the system of race.

In his dissent on this decision, Justice William Brennan stated forthrightly a sense of lament and frustration at this clear choice of race over equality.

We ignore [McCleskey] at our peril, for we remain imprisoned by the past as long as we deny its influence in the present. It is tempting to pretend that minorities on death row share a fate in no way connected to our own, that our treatment of them sounds no echoes beyond the chambers in which they die. Such an illusion is ultimately corrosive,

for the reverberations of injustice are not so easily confined....The way in which we choose who will die reveals
the depth of moral commitment among the living (*Char-
leston Gazette*, May 26, 1987, p. A-7).

Having seen how the death penalty has been used and continues to be used, Justice Harry Blackmun changed his position
after almost twenty-five years and announced that he would no
longer vote for the death penalty. Until his retirement from the
Court in 1994, he was the only judge who openly opposed it on
the Supreme Court.

The problems in African-American communities are the central focus of current political debate. Whether it is crime, education, welfare, family values, drugs, jobs, or violence, the society
continues to focus on African-American life. There are two levels
to this kind of scrutiny, each of which will be examined more
closely in the next chapter. The first level is to assert that African-American communities are *the* problem facing our society.
From the Declaration of Independence's "We hold these truths
to be self-evident: that all men are created equal" to Jefferson's
"firebell in the night" to Lincoln's "government of the people"
to Martin Luther King, Jr.'s, "I have a dream," to Malcolm X's
"nightmare," our society has been obsessed with race and its
consequent problems. By making race the central part of our
identity in the United States, we have guaranteed that it will be
the center of our lives, that it will always be present, first and
foremost. The lives of African-American people are always under the microscope in our society. They are studied and analyzed, and solutions are given for their problems. It is rare,
however, for white people to be studied and analyzed, for white
people believe that their culture is normative. The first level of
scrutiny consists of blaming African-Americans for their condition of oppression.

The second level is to admit the obvious—African-American
people face great problems in this society. Although there has
been a great expansion of the black middle class because of the
human rights movement of the 1960s, a vastly disproportionate
black population still lives in poverty. More black men are in the
clutches of the law enforcement system than in college. Chronic

unemployment and many other immense problems must be addressed. The manner in which they are addressed will depend on how we assign the responsibility for them.

White people believe that most of the barriers of race have been eliminated through the civil rights movement. If there are continuing problems in the black community, the feeling of white people is that race is not as much a deterrent to black progress as are "the personal inadequacies of black people."* We have thus returned to the post-Reconstruction position: African-Americans are to blame for the problems that they now face. The role of the system of race is largely ignored. This is almost the exact stance white society took in post-Reconstruction, and its fruits are bitter. Its fruits are the denial of equality in favor of race and the continuing oppression of people of darker color, all the while blaming them for their plight. Just as in post-Reconstruction, rather than understanding the continuing power of race, we have chosen to blame African-Americans for the problems of racism.

---

* Douglas Glasgow, *The Black Underclass* (New York: Vintage Books, 1981), p. 73.

CHAPTER 4

The American Nightmare

The power of race and racism is deeply embedded in our society. As a result, people of darker color, especially African-Americans, are seen and treated as second-class citizens. The lack of access to power, the inequality of opportunity, and the injustices they suffer are interpreted by society as inherent in the character and culture of black people rather than inherent in the system of race. To examine manifestations of the system of race in this way is not to absolve the African-American community of all responsibility, but to recognize the truth that the system of race is central to the destiny and life of all people in this country, especially people of darker color—and most especially African-American people. No one is innocent, especially white people. White people have set up the system of race, and we must come to realize how much we benefit from it and how much we avoid acknowledging its existence.

White people have a sense of this struggle. Patrick Buchanan, who was a headline speaker at the Republican convention in August 1992, laid out the struggle for white people in blunt terms: "We must take back our cities, take back our culture, take back our country." It is clear that the "we" are the white people, who established the system of race and now want to reestablish it, despite the gains of the civil rights movement. This is the American nightmare: white people unwilling to give up the system of race and black people forced to take the blame for it.

We will now look at four areas in which the struggle takes place: poverty, family values, education, and law enforcement.

Not every African-American family is poor. This cannot be emphasized enough because white people have a large stake in being able to connect poverty with the life and culture of black people. There is a deliberate misconception that all black people are poor or that black culture tends toward poverty. This is deliberate because the system of race demands that we make the equation of black equals poor. White people have been conditioned to accept that black people have less worth than white people and, therefore, that poverty is a natural part of black culture. The system of race is heavily invested in cultivating demeaning images of African-Americans, and the current idea that African-Americans tend toward poverty because of their behavior is only the most recent version of the story.

Having said that, however, it must also be said that many African-Americans continue to be poor. Some 37 percent make less than $15,000 per year. The 1990 census figures show that 44.8 percent of all African-American children live in poverty. Many more black people are poor than their ratio of population (12 percent) should reflect. Why are so many poor? The answer may be complex, but it boils down to either/or. Either black people tend toward poverty because of their character as a people, or their disproportionate poverty is a manifestation of the system of race. This question of poverty reflects the dualism that DuBois lifted up a hundred years ago. To be an African-American is to have a dual nature. To be an African is to affirm your humanity and possibility; to be an American is to acknowledge the power of the system of race that seeks to crush you. In this dualism, African-American people are damned if they do and damned if they don't. If they "succeed" in the culture, it is used as evidence that there is no system of race. If they do not succeed and are crushed by despair, poverty, prison, or addiction, it is used as evidence that African-American people are not quite the human beings that white people are. This dualism is at work in the issue of poverty.

There are more poor white families than black families in the United States. In 1985, as reported by the American Enterprise Institute in Washington, the ratio was 5 to 2. In sheer numbers, then, family poverty is a white problem, indeed a national problem. Yet, our society sees poverty as primarily a "nonwhite" problem. The contradiction of these two facts should never be forgotten: Poverty is a national problem, but our society sees it only as a "nonwhite" problem. The reason given for this myopia is that a disproportionate number of black families are poor. The real reason is that white people want to see poverty as an inherent characteristic of being black. We want to believe that black people choose to be poor.

Over the past thirty years, our society has chosen to deal with the "discovery" of poverty in our midst through a welfare program. The meaning of the word *welfare* has undergone an interesting transformation. Promoting the general welfare is one of the six purposes for forming the governmental structure of the United States cited in the Preamble to the Constitution. In this sense, all U.S. citizens are on welfare. In our time, however, welfare has come to mean only the poor, chiefly the black poor. Welfare reform is a central political issue throughout the nation. A CBS/*New York Times* poll (July 25, 1992, p. A-13) revealed intentions in welfare reform. When the question was asked, "Are we spending too little, too much, or just about enough on welfare?" 44 percent said too much, 27 percent enough, and 23 percent too little. When the question was rephrased by replacing "welfare" with "assistance to the poor," the answers shifted dramatically—64 percent said too little, 13 percent too much, and 16 percent enough. This is stunning evidence that welfare has come to mean not the general population, as the Preamble to the Constitution states, but only a segment of the population, namely the "nonwhite" poor.

Further evidence for using welfare reform as an attack on black people is found in *The New Consensus on Family Welfare*, published in 1988 by the American Enterprise Institute, a conservative think tank in Washington, D.C. Its claim is that many of those currently on welfare are there only because their own behavior has put them there.

> A significant proportion of those who fall into poverty today do so through changes in family status: divorce, separation, or having a child out of wedlock. These are

clearly matters of personal responsibility....At the heart of the poverty problem in 1987 is, then, the problem of behavioral dependency (pp. 13, 72).

One could argue whether or not dependency is a problem created by the welfare system, but that argument is not the point of *The New Consensus.* Its point is to assert that "behavioral dependency" is a black problem, not a white problem. The authors even go so far as to make the astonishing assertion that white poverty does not imply "behavioral dependency," while black poverty does.

Poor white children in rural areas are probably not suffering under the harsh conditions most poor black children meet in urban areas. Although they belong to families whose incomes fall below the poverty line, their condition may seem relatively close to that of many of their non-poor companions. By contrast, poor black children are concentrated in areas where other hazards may be worse than falling below the official poverty line. To be below the poverty line in rural areas of Utah, Kansas, or Maine may not imply dependency or dysfunction, but below-poverty living in center-city Chicago, Cleveland, or New York often does (p. 56).

Why would the authors make such a strange and unsupportable distinction between white poverty and black poverty? The reason is that it is important for the system of race to establish the belief that white poverty is accidental but black poverty is inherent. Thus, black people will be seen as those who are "behaviorally dependent" on society, while white people are not. Once this is understood, the reason behind the current drive for welfare reform becomes clearer: It is a way to attack black people. It is no coincidence that welfare reform is joining Willie Horton as the code for conjuring up the fears and anxieties of white people.

Increasingly, states are passing laws that cut benefits for the poor and force them into "workfare." It is a script written and predicated on the system of race, as Michael Novak and his associate state in the concluding pages of *The New Consensus*: "The nation must not be concerned if low income results from a voluntary choice" (p. 95). In other words, we can forget about the black poor. The black families who are cut loose in their poverty are behaviorally dependent and thus *chose* their poverty. We need not be concerned about them because their poverty is a personal choice.

There is a second line of attack on the welfare system. This approach asserts that the purpose of the welfare system is to keep as many black people as possible at a subsistence level. Though many black scholars have agreed with this approach, none has been more relentless than Douglas Glasgow in *The Black Underclass*, published in 1980. In blunt fashion, Glasgow attacks the welfare system as a way of controlling black people.

> In the absence of any realistic alternative, they remain at the mercy of those who manipulate these programs, who ostensibly are responding to the needs of the poor but whose real concern is with regulating, controlling, and maintaining the poor (p. 182).

Glasgow also attacks the welfare system for encouraging dependency among black people who are poor. Whereas the American Enterprise Institute sees this behavioral dependency as endemic to black people, Glasgow sees it as a way of keeping black people from reaching their full potential. It "leads to the delusion that society will, if reminded enough, eventually provide a public assistance program capable of adequately supporting an individual and his or her family. Nothing is less likely" (p. 183). This approach understands the welfare system to be an opiate of the people, a way of perpetuating black poverty by making black people feel grateful for the handouts. At the same time it takes away their dignity by calling them lazy for taking the handouts.

One of the reasons the welfare system became debilitating is that its benefits never have been high enough to get a majority of people out of poverty. Even today, only fourteen states provide as much as 80 percent of the official poverty level (*New York Times*, July 25, 1992, p. A-13). No state provides a financial level of support that will allow a family to survive. The very people who are supposed to be helped by the welfare system often become those brought back into a "slave" mentality by it. The welfare system also fails because it sees poverty as related to black life. As Glasgow has noted, the nation sees only "pockets of poverty" rather than seeing poverty as pandemic to our society. The welfare system is a failure because it fails to take into account the system of race.

It must be emphasized again that not all African-Americans are poor. This cannot be repeated often enough, because our society strives to make the connection that black equals poor. The Children's Defense Fund released statistics in 1991 that are stunning because they fly so completely in the face of this commonly held belief. Of the 12 million poor children in this country, only 10 percent are urban, black, and living with a mother on welfare. One of the great successes of the civil rights movement has been the expansion of the black middle class. Yet, the continuing power of the system of race means that many black people remain in poverty. Until we recognize the connection between poverty and the system of race (rather than the false connection between poverty and being black), attempts to reform the welfare system will prove futile.

What, then, can be said about the current welfare system? First, despite the white desire to see welfare as proof that behavioral dependency is inherent in black life, welfare has helped some people move out of poverty. Even today, as we moan about the perpetuation of generations of black people on welfare, there are more success stories than failures. Because of the hard work of poor families, more than half of all AFDC (Aid to Families with Dependent Children) families leave the welfare rolls before their third year on the program (Hacker, p. 85). Second, it must be stressed that until the connection between welfare and the system of race is acknowledged, reform efforts will only continue to perpetuate black poverty while blaming black people for it, whether it is called welfare, workfare, segregation, or slavery.

Third, and perhaps most important, we must recognize that the scene has shifted in the system of race. We have wanted to keep colored people poor so that they would be a source of cheap labor. This was the purpose of slavery and the segregation that followed Reconstruction. As this century closes, however, the mechanization of agriculture and the shipping of cheap labor jobs overseas has made the presence of cheap laborers less necessary. Some cheap labor is still necessary. That is why we have labor pools and a huge homeless population of black men—they provide a pool of cheap labor. The overall questions of the welfare system and poverty are really questions that this society faces as it considers its low-income African-American members: are they still needed as a source of cheap labor? If not, what will happen to them? Can they finally be treated as equal partners in society, with dignity that they deserve as human beings? The sole purpose of bringing people of African descent to this country was to have cheap labor. The system of race was built for this purpose. If they are no longer needed as cheap labor, and if the whites who control society do not want African-Americans as equal partners, what will happen to low-income African-Americans? What will happen to all of us? These questions are disturbing and frightening because they demand that we rethink some very fundamental issues concerning the function of race.

The desire to see poverty as a condition of black life is an image we must keep before us. There is a strong desire to see black people and black life at the root of many of the problems we face as a culture. Whether it is crime, education, decay of the cities, or lack of productivity, there is a push to see African-American people as the cause. In blaming African-American people for the problems of society, we are following a long tradition in this country: We are exonerating the system of race by assigning responsibility for it to people of darker color, especially African-Americans. Under this image, we will look at the other three areas: family values, education, and law enforcement.

There is a strong movement to see black life as helpless and hopeless: absent fathers, promiscuous women and girls, drug addicts, slums, crime, laziness, and welfare dependency. Yet, we dare not underestimate how much this list of images is related to the system of race. This perception of hopeless black life was essential to reestablishing slavery and legal segregation following Reconstruction. It is essential now if white society has its way in seeking to repudiate the gains of the civil rights movement, which established firm ground for a black middle class and lifted up the primacy of the idea of equality over the idea of race.

This list of images of black life has led us to a central issue for the 1992 and 1994 elections: family values. Just as "behavioral dependency" is code language for "blacks are lazy," so "family values" is code for "blacks don't care about family structure." When Dan Quayle made his famous May 18, 1992, speech about family values in San Francisco, the media coverage centered on his attack on the television show "Murphy Brown." Overlooked in this coverage, however, was Quayle's central theme: The Los Angeles riots and the poverty in the inner cities were caused by a collapse in family values. Indeed, in a clever but extremely disturbing turn of phrase, Quayle insisted that there was a "poverty of values gripping our inner cities." Here, Quayle used three code words for black life without ever explicitly using the language of race: "poverty" (seen as a condition of black life), "values" (the assertion that the black family has collapsed), and "inner cities" (only black people live there). It should be much clearer now why studies of poverty want to separate black poverty from white poverty. White poverty is seen as accidental; black poverty is seen as inherent in being black.

The stability of the black family has been the center of numerous conferences, articles, and documentaries. This is not accidental—it is designed to reinforce the system of race that insists that black people and black families are unstable, unreliable, and unworthy of support. Rarely, if ever, is it mentioned that changes in the black family are part of a national trend in family structure. The Bureau of Labor statistics for 1988 indicated that the "ideal" family of the 1950s (father as breadwinner, mother staying home with children) represented only 8 percent of *all* American families. The 1990 Census indicated that this percentage continues to drop. The percentage of this "ideal" family is now down to about 3 percent, with one-third of *all* families headed by a single parent. Hacker notes this trend and points out that the ratio for families headed by women has remained remarkably stable between black families and white families over the last forty years, a ratio of 3:2 (p. 68). In other words, the family values debate ought not to become code language for race. It reflects *national* trends, not black trends.

Having said this, it must also be noted that much of the instability in black families originates in the fact that they are constantly under attack. More accurately stated, it is the black male who is under attack. Hacker reports statistics from 1990 that show that 56.2 percent of all black households are headed by women (p. 68). On every institutional level, the black male is an endangered species. From the former Fulton County Commission chairman who was unable to get a conventional home improvement bank loan to the young teenager pushed into a life of crime, the way for black males in the system of race is treacherous indeed. Why is this? Historically, it has been clear that keeping the black male in chaos is essential to maintaining the system of race. For instance, it is no accident that welfare requirements state that no able-bodied father can be living in the household if the family is to receive AFDC benefits. Where, then, is the father to live? It is an automatic and calculated formula for chaos.

Glasgow puts it bluntly: "Why do so many inner-city Black males fail to negotiate the system, and why is this pattern of failure so widespread?" (p. 73). How one answers this question determines whether one will accept the system of race or reject it. The overwhelming answer from our society in the last two decades has been that the answer is in the problems of black culture. Glasgow sums up this answer well:

An entirely new nomenclature was developed to describe this condition. We heard not only about the "disadvantaged" and the "culturally deprived" but about "deficit character," "thwarted characterological development" (most often hypothesized as stemming from years of deprivation) and the "culture of poverty." Instead of directing major effort to opening up economic opportunity—to jobs, new careers, union membership, on-the-job training, and up-grading programs—social planners suggested an emphasis on psychosocial rehabilitative programs.…The underlying assumption of this approach was that racism was not as important a deterrent to Black progress as were the personal inadequacies with which Blacks were saddled (p. 73).

If this sounds amazingly similar to post-Reconstruction thinking, that should be no surprise. The same methods are being used now to attack African-Americans and blame them for the attack. Few voices in the mainstream culture are willing to dispute what has come to be regarded as conventional truth: What is needed is not an attack on the system of race but a "remedial" approach for black people who have fallen behind because of their inadequacies.

White moderates, white liberals, and some black folks in our culture have now begun to agree that the black poor are *causing* racism, instead of racism causing black poverty. As in post-Reconstruction, the approach is to make the continuing oppression of African-Americans their responsibility. It is as if Booker T. Washington were addressing the Olympic convention in Atlanta in 1995 rather than the Cotton States Exposition in Atlanta in 1895: Only when black people are ready will they receive equal rights and equal access to opportunity. Of course, they will never be ready. To gain further insight into this system that seeks to guarantee failure for African-Americans, we now turn from family values to two other institutions that pervade black life: education and law enforcement.

Education is central for two reasons. First, it is the place where black youth encounter the system of race at an early age. Second, it is one of the systems in which the modern civil rights movement began. In *Brown v. Board of Education* (1954), the Supreme Court ruled that the separate but equal doctrine of 1896 violated the Constitution in regard to public education. Yet more than forty years after *Brown,* 63.3 percent of all black children attend segregated schools, largely because of white flight (Hacker, p. 162). It appears that the vast majority of white people simply will not tolerate sending their children to school with black children. School system after school system has abandoned integration efforts; the Supreme Court's ruling of 1992 in the DeKalb County, Georgia, case (cited in Chapter 3) will further reinforce that resignation.

We must be careful here to assert the fundamental issue of desegregation. The issue is not that the "deprived" black child must sit beside the more intelligent white child to gain greatness from white culture and thus be lifted up. The issue is that the money and energy of the school systems follow the white children because the systems are white controlled. The concept of separate but equal was thrown out in 1954 precisely for this reason. There is no possibility that a separate system for people of darker color will receive the same attention and funding as a system for white people. It is simply impossible under the system of race. It is what we have observed in so many of our inner cities—as whites flee and the schools become segregated, there is inattention and then decay in what have become black schools. Why? The reason is not that black people are incapable but that the energy and money of the system have fled with the white children.

When some white energy returns or stays, it often is part of an approach that is deadly to black children: remedial learning. Rather than seeing black children as students who have exciting potential and who have learned to survive in a hostile culture, the white-controlled educational systems see black children as deprived, unstable, and unwilling-to-learn students who need to remedy their individual or cultural deficit. The remedy that is given is an assault on black life and black culture. Hacker summarizes it well.

That black children have not been well served by the schools hardly needs recounting. In the view of growing numbers of black educators, the reasons are inherently racial. In all parts of the country, as they see it, school systems are organized and administered by white officials who have little understanding of the needs of black children. Even in schools that have black principals and are staffed largely by black teachers, state rules shape most of the curriculum, often limiting the choice of books and imposing uniform testing. To a casual visitor, such a school may seem "all black." Yet further observation reveals the influence of white power and authority. Saddest of all, abilities and aspirations of black children often remain unrecognized, if not discouraged or destroyed (pp. 170-71).

Glasgow made this same point eleven years earlier.

Much of this research had an underlying premise that being Black (and poor) was directly related to educational under-achievement. Because educators and legislators, whether consciously or unconsciously, believed this premise was fact, they developed and supported numerous programs that sought to supplement and compensate for what was assumed to be either missing or insufficient ingredients in the ghetto youths' life (pp. 54-55).

The important point is that the abilities of African-American children go unrecognized in the educational system. The extraordinary ability of African-American culture to survive and even thrive in the hostile environment of the system of race is not lifted up. What if the school systems celebrated the humanity and remarkable resiliency of African-American culture? What if we recognized the ability to negotiate the hostile systems, if we recognized the astonishing power of the extended family to help children survive? Then the talk about family values would have meaning other than race; the focus of remedial learning would not be black culture but white culture. To change this focus, however, would require that the system of race be honestly acknowledged, confronted, and finally dismantled.

The encounter of black children, especially black males, with our educational system is an encounter that tells them that something is wrong with them and with their culture. Every part of the educational system is designed to tell black children a terrible lie: You are basically bad, and your culture is basically bad. Until this fundamental orientation is confronted, there will be little hope for significant change in the school system. It is a depressing process: White society seeks to maintain the system of race by destroying the self-concept of black children who enter the educational systems. It is no wonder that there is so little recognized achievement and there are so many dropouts in the segregated black schools. When black children fail to live up to the white norm, white people feel reaffirmed in the system of race. When black youth drop out of school, the third institution—law enforcement—awaits them, if they have not already encountered it.

It is in the law enforcement system that the violence whites have used for centuries to maintain the system of race emerges most blatantly. Sometimes it is controlled violence. As in the case of Rodney King (and many thousands of others whose assaults were not caught on videotape), the violence is often uncontrolled. The power of race is seen most clearly in the law enforcement system.

There is no better place to start than with the use of Willie Horton in the 1988 presidential election. Horton was an African-American man sentenced to prison in Massachusetts for murder. During Michael Dukakis's term as governor of that state, Horton was allowed to leave prison through a furlough program. During one such furlough, he fled the state, went to Maryland, broke into the home of a white couple, and raped the woman. A black man, convicted of murder, let out of prison by "soft" liberals, attacked and raped a white woman. Republicans used Horton's story to demonstrate that Dukakis and the Democrats were soft on crime—especially black crime. The image was that if Dukakis were elected, the savagery of black men would be loosed on white women.

Our culture is obsessed with crime. It is the lead story on all television news programs, and we are all afraid. We are not obsessed with all crime, however. There has been very little outcry about those who robbed and pilfered billions in the savings-and-loans scandals (most if not all of whom were white males). The crime with which our society is obsessed is "street crime"—assaults, robberies, rape, and murder. This is known as—or is code language for—"black crime" because a disproportionate number of people convicted of these offenses are black men. We must remember that I said that a disproportionate number of people *convicted* for these crimes are black. Because we clear only about 10 percent of the crimes reported, we have no idea who is *committing* the other 90 percent. One would think that the dynamics of this situation would be obvious.

White society wants to see black men as savage and criminal, and, therefore, great energy is put into arresting, convicting, and imprisoning black men. The reasons black men commit so many of these crimes should also be obvious: The system of race produces unemployment, anger and rage, and self-destructive behavior. Our society chooses to overlook these dynamics to conclude that black men are more prone to violent crime because of a deficit in black life. Chad G. Glover, a black writer, reflected on this approach in his thoughts about being stopped by the police in Ohio because he allegedly fit the description of a robber.

> The run-in with Kent's finest was a not-too-subtle re-
> minder that when all is said and done, I am a nigger, and
> not a college student, a future journalist or even an Ameri-
> can. To almost all cops and most of society, I am a criminal
> who happens not to have committed his first crime.
>
> The tragedy isn't that I was inconvenienced for a half
> hour or even that I felt violated. The true horror of this
> story is that I thought I was different. Special. Like, if I get
> good enough grades, a good enough job or a nice enough
> car, then America will see me differently and stop asking
> me to "Spread'em" (*Essence Magazine*, Sept. 1994, p. 48).

This approach to black males follows them throughout their lives. It is the job of the law enforcement system, especially the police, to keep the black boys, black youth, and black men in line—to seek to control the rage. There is rage, and there is violence. There is violence against white people, but there is even more black-on-black violence. The leading cause of death for black youth is homicide by other black youth. Is the violence generated by the system of race, or is it generated by a deficit in the culture of African-American people? For most white people, the answer is to be found in a little bit of racism and a whole lot of deficit in African-American culture. White people move quickly to believe that there is something disturbing, something deficient in black males. As Hacker indicates, street crime is so threatening to whites because it forces us to see that we can still be terrorized by a group deemed to be worth less than we are (p. 188).

Nowhere is this seen more clearly than in the current debate in the uproar over violence. The President of the United States unveiled a series of public service announcements in March 1994, decrying the violence in our culture. There is no doubt that violence has taken on a random nature and that it claims young black males as its chief victims. This must be stopped, and all communities—black and white, rich and poor—must play a part in changing it. The laws being passed by state legislatures for more prisons and harsher prison sentences are not the answer, however. We will not find the real answer until we understand how much the system of race is embedded in the debate.

The clearest example of the power of race comes from one of the standard-bearers of the system of race, James Q. Wilson. In response to the first Rodney King verdict and the rebellions that followed, Wilson wrote an article originally printed in the *Wall Street Journal* that indicated both how powerful the system of race is and how reluctant whites are to admit its power.

But if racist thinking has declined, why are relations between the races so bad? Why has Los Angeles, like many other cities, become more segregated residentially today than it was in 1965? Why do so many whites who cannot be called racists in any fair meaning of the word so often treat blacks warily or react to their proposals with neglect or unease? Fear. Whites are afraid of young black males (and of young Latino males). It is not racism that keeps whites from exploring black neighborhoods, it is fear. It is not racism that leads white parents to pull their children out of schools with many black students, it is fear. Fear of crime, of drugs, of gangs, of violence.

Reducing poverty, ending racism, creating jobs and improving schooling are all good things to do, whether or not they prevent crimes or riots. But the problem our big cities face runs far deeper. There is an underclass, and though many races are found among it and it accounts for only a strong fraction of the black community, it is perceived to be a black phenomenon. So long as black men commit violent crimes at a rate that is six to eight times higher than the rate found among whites, that perception will persist. And as long as that perception persists, fear will heighten our anxieties and erode our civility (*Memphis Commercial Appeal,* May 10, 1992, p. B-7).

It is interesting that Wilson says it is not racism but fear that keeps whites in flight from blacks. Fear is an integral part of racism, and it is testimony to the desire of whites to deny racism that Wilson goes through such mental gymnastics to disavow racism. Even more interesting is how easily Wilson dismisses the list of things that would clearly reduce crime, as if it were a matter of picking dandelions on a sunny day: "Reducing poverty, ending racism, creating jobs and improving schools are all good things to do...*But*..." The "but" in Wilson's case is the "underclass," a group of black males so intractable that none of the remedies listed above would change them. Wilson clearly wants to establish an essential tenet for white people who cannot acknowledge the power of race: There is something fundamentally wrong with black people, something so wrong that no matter what steps are taken by whites to implement equality, black people *still* could not handle equality.

From Wilson's point of view, fear of black males is not racism—it is natural because black males tend to be criminals, even if poverty were eliminated, racism dismantled, good jobs available for everyone, and quality education given to all. Black people still would be unable to handle all this. The system of race is not the problem, says Wilson: The inadequacy, indeed the savagery, of black people is the problem. Lest this seems overblown, it must be noted here that Wilson is not an Aryan nation's rebel hiding in the mountains of the Northwest. He is a professor of management and public policy at UCLA (the University of California, Los Angeles), and he was one of the intellectuals with whom Dan Quayle met before crafting his San Francisco speech connecting poverty and oppression in Los Angeles with the breakdown of family values. For Wilson and Quayle and many other whites (and some blacks), a few minor changes may have to be made in white society to help African-Americans; but for these leaders, the biggest problem is the big "But." That "but" is what whites see as the inherent inadequacy and inequality of black people and black culture. From this point of view, what needs change is not white culture *but* black culture.

Understanding this white point of view is essential if we are to gain insight into how the system of race impacts law enforcement and crime control. To say this is not to deny that black people have responsibility for crimes they commit. They are well aware of it, and indeed many black leaders see violent crime as a greater threat to them than racism. We must be very careful here, however. The desire to remove whites from responsibility for racism is so great that we take a dangerous step if we divorce the rage in the black community from the racism in our society. The rage is fueled by the racism—we must always keep that before us. To seek to deal with violence in the black community by building more jails and prisons is to misunderstand the roots of the rage. The threat of incarceration will not diminish black rage—loosening the bonds of racism will. This is the approach we must take.

In this context, we can return to crime control. As always in the system of race, it is difficult to prove that a racist intent drives the police and the court system. The results, however, are difficult to dispute. The results indicate that the primary function of the criminal justice system is not to respond to crime or even to punish criminals.

The results indicate that the primary function of this system is to respond to and punish crime committed by those seen as threats to our way of life. This includes and targets black males, most especially. Again, it is difficult to prove intent, but the results of our "lock-them-up" mentality of the 1980s (which has extended into the 1990s) is clear. None of the laws imposing mandatory sentences passed during this time specifically targeted black people and other people of darker color. This would have been constitutionally illegal. Yet the enforcement of many laws has demonstrated the impetus that lay behind them. For instance, a federal court in St. Louis declared a 1986 federal law concerning crack cocaine to be unconstitutional because it was pervaded "with inhumanity and injustice" in regard to race. Why did it do this? Because 97 percent of those sentenced under this law were black or Hispanic. Another liberal, "soft-on-crime" court? No, Senior Judge Clyde Cahill indicated that it was the first time in his twenty-year tenure that he had even considered invalidating a law. He did so because he found that the actions of lawmakers and prosecutors were

> influenced and motivated by unconscious racism, causing great harm and injury to black defendants because of their race, inasmuch as whites are rarely arrested, prosecuted or convicted for crack cocaine offenses (*Atlanta Constitution*, Feb. 19, 1994, p. A-1).

In 1981 and 1982, I was a staff member of the Southern Coalition on Jails and Prisons, and my work there gave me insight into this process. Part of my job was to work for prison reform in the state legislature. My work with the legislature was based on the premise that the prison system was a response to crime. My job was to help convince legislators that there were demonstrably effective alternatives to incarceration that were much less costly than prisons. In a time when the nation was demanding lower taxes, I agreed with our staff's assumption that a demonstration of cost savings to the state by the use of alternatives to prison would result in the increased use of these alternatives and a decreased use of prison cells. I was rudely awakened to discover that cost was not a particularly important issue concerning incarceration because prisons are not used as a response to crime in our society.

We pulled together a commission of leading citizens in the legislature, law enforcement, and the judicial system for the purpose of examining the feasibility of alternatives to incarceration. During these meetings, it was made clear to us that there was little desire to move to alternatives, even if they cost less and worked better in the long run. The public wanted those convicted of crimes to be locked up, no matter the cost. At the heart of this desire is race.

Statistics bear this out. In 1970, whites were 60.5 percent of the prison population, and people of darker color were 39.5 percent. In 1986, the reverse was true—39.6 percent were white and 60.4 percent of the people were of darker color. During this same period, the increase in the number of prisoners was phenomenal. In 1968, the prison population in the United States was 188,000. By 1981, it had reached 338,000. By 1991 it had doubled to 600,000, giving our nation the highest rate of incarceration in the world—higher than South Africa, higher than the former Soviet Union (as reported in the Bureau of Justice Statistics Bulletin, 1991). Why has prison population doubled in the last decade, even though the crime rate has stayed approximately the same? The reason is that the law enforcement system is not a response to crime but to the systems of race and class.

Several of my black church members have male family members in prison. They consistently refer to prison as the "chain gang." I thought that this reference was a quaint euphemism from their rural roots until I realized the significance of the word *chain*. Slavery was not totally abolished in the Thirteenth Amendment. It was abolished "except as a punishment for crime whereof the party shall have been duly convicted." Thus, the chains of prison are connected to the chains of slavery. These African-American families knew much more than I did about the roots of the current prison system which, for them, is seen as a substitute for the chains of slavery.

One wonders where this will all end. At present there is no end in sight except more prisons, more people of darker color in those prisons, more violence, and more white people filled with fear (but not racism, according to James Q. Wilson!).

I will offer a final graphic example of how our law enforcement system is used to maintain the system of race through violence. In August 1992, Michael Milken, the junk bond dealer who was sentenced to ten years in prison for fraud, had his sentence reduced to two years by a federal judge. There was a mild outcry that a white "white-collar" criminal was treated less harshly than black men convicted of street crimes. Mike Royko, in his nationally syndicated column, answered for white people and for the system of race in a column called "Milken: A Crook to Admire." In it, Royko states that we need Milken's brilliance because he is well-educated and committed to excellence. Royko gets to his real point as he ends the column.

But I've known many white-collar criminals. I've also known many dirty-collar criminals. And given a choice,

I'd rather run into Michael Milken in a dark alley than some guy with missing teeth, hair growing out of his forehead and drool on his chin….I'll present one more argument in Milken's behalf.

Your daughter comes home with two men. She says: "Mom, Dad, I am in love with both of these fellows. But I can't decide which one I will marry.

"Edward, here, has an MBA and fine table manners and is becoming rich on Wall Street. However, he has a character flaw. He is greedy and might be breaking some financial laws.

"Louie, here, quit school for a career holding up all-night convenience stores, and he also moonlights as a mugger, specializing in stomping old people in the park.

"So, which one do you want as a son-in-law?"

I rest my case (Savannah *Evening News*, Aug. 11, 1992, p. A-6).

It is not too difficult to discern the skin color of the guy with the missing teeth. Just in case we are unsure, Royko gives us the most important clue of all as far as the system of race is concerned by asking his readers, Which one would you want your daughter to marry?

In all four of the systems discussed above—welfare, poverty, education, and law enforcement—the system of race operates to destroy the humanity of people of darker color, especially African-Americans, while blaming these same people for their own demise. Rather than confronting the system of race as the civil rights movement has asked us to do, we have chosen to return to the methods of post-Reconstruction, in which the system of race is reasserted by repudiating the human rights gains of the civil rights movement. The white response has produced fruits that are depressing and oppressing.

These fruits are twofold. First, those who have claimed the name white are seen as normal and as absolved from culpability in regard to the system of race. White people, then, are shocked when it is claimed that we are racist and that we still benefit from the system of race. Many of us white people are genuinely shocked at this revelation because we have been led to believe—

and we have wanted to believe—that the system of race is no longer important. To be confronted with the claim that our whiteness is arbitrary and racist is genuinely disturbing—it produces guilt and denial. We feel cut adrift, and we usually return to the dynamics of the system of race—we are no longer participants in racism, but when confronted by examples of a lack of opportunity or a lack of justice for people of darker color, we say it is their fault and their responsibility.

The second fruit is a powerful, negative self-image for people of darker color, especially African-American people. The rage and despair in their communities have to do with this profound consequence of the system of race: White is good, and black is bad. This statement asserts a fundamental dynamic of American life that white people want so much to forget: The system of race still has great power, and part of its power is to produce a self-hatred in people of darker color. Much of the struggle of people of darker color in this society is to find ways to affirm their humanity so that they will not run this race in vain.

We have seen a powerful and encouraging emergence of black consciousness and affirmation of black life in the last thirty years—a testimony to the power and creativity of African-Americans. It seems so strong in the present that it seems impossible to return to the days of self-hatred that Malcolm X lifted up. Yet we must not forget the past. There were also strong and eloquent voices in the black community after Reconstruction: W. E. B. DuBois, Ida B. Wells, Monroe Trotter, Thomas Fortune, Alexander Crummell, Henry M. Turner, and many others. These dynamic witnesses were overwhelmed by the tidal wave of race. Many of their voices were forgotten and lost, although we are rediscovering them in our time. It is not a lack of black voices that is the problem—it is a lack of white voices who speak for equality. White voices speak more and more for the system of race; and as much as we wish that black people would not accept the denigrating white voices, Glasgow reminds us in blunt fashion about the power of the system of race to overwhelm black culture.

No fanciful detention centers "secretly being built to harbor niggers" could be worse than the reality of the modern ghetto trap. The resentment originally generated by the mass white exodus has long since subsided, and for at least ten years the central city has been all Black. Many of the encounters, tensions, and survival struggles involve Blacks with Blacks. The truth is that no one is spared the destructive consequences of ghetto living. The never-ending cycle goes something like this: Being broke, hustling, jiving, stealing, rapping, bailing; a fight, a bust, some time; no job, lost a job, a no-paying job; a lady, a baby, some weight; some wine, some grass, a pill; no ride, lost pride, man going down, slipping fast, can't see where to make it; I've tried, almost died, ready now for almost anything (p. 104).

White is good; black is bad. It is the fundamental divide of our society that has been with us from the European beginning of this nation.

CHAPTER 5

"Been in the Storm So Long"*

The system of race is part of the daily existence of people of darker color, especially African-Americans. It is a daily encounter whether one is an integrationist or a separatist or one who has a good job or who is desperately poor. The system of race is a daily storm that people of darker color must endure.

White people, on the other hand, have trouble understanding this daily occurrence and even have trouble hearing it. We who claim the name white are often oblivious to the system of race and how it works. Unless we place ourselves in a position to encounter it, we will not be constantly reminded of its existence. This is how it is supposed to be—white people are normal and are at the top of the hierarchy of race, so we do not even have to think about it. When people of darker color speak about the power of race, white people have trouble believing their experience and their feelings. We tell them that they are wrong, that their feelings come from some other source. We tell them that they are paranoid, that they have misunderstood the situation, or that they don't understand how life works. We who are white are stunned and angered when black people speak about race because we have been taught to believe that the system of race no longer exists. When black people describe racism, it is clear to us that they have a chip on their shoulders and don't under-

_____

* From the nineteenth-century spiritual "Been in the Storm So Long."

stand. This gap in experience is part of the great divide: Black people experience it daily; white people rarely get a glimpse of it. In this chapter, we will seek to share insight concerning the meaning of being black in this culture.

As a white person, and as a white male especially, I enter this discussion with great trepidation. After four chapters describing the great divide of race in which we who claim the name "white" seek to determine and shape the reality of the lives of all those we call "nonwhite," now I am presuming to describe what it means to be black. It is a huge presumption, and I urge all readers to take it for what it is: a great leap with many dangers, and one small step for a white man. Read this as the beginning of a journey, not the end. It is attempted only to indicate how wide the gap is between understandings of race, and this attempt may only serve to verify that! Many better resources are available, and one of them, Inez Fleming, will express her understanding later in this chapter. I urge each reader to consult other resources for more definitive interpretations, with the annotated bibliography as a starting place (see p. 173 below).

If I have such reservations about describing a bit of what I think it means to be black in this culture, why do it? Why not leave it to those who are called "black"? While my perceptions are undoubtedly skewed, I lift them up in hopes of opening a dialogue on race, a dialogue that so often goes unspoken or even denied. I write not as a mediator for black people but as a white man trying to come to terms with the power of race.

Although people called black and other people of darker color in this society are human beings—they feel like people and act like people—they live in a society that tells them that they are not human in the same way white people are human. They are told that there is a vast gap between them and white people, that something is wrong with them and their culture. This dissonance produces great tensions in people of darker color. It makes them want to hide their humanity and their culture from white people. It makes them tend to disengage from white people. It produces great anger and frustration and a dualism born of the need to live as a human beings in a world that tells them they are not human beings.

This dualism is nothing new for people of darker color. It is

at the heart of their experience, and no one lifted it up better than
W. E. B. DuBois:

> One feels his two-ness—an American, a Negro, two souls,
> two thoughts, two unreconciled strivings, two warring
> ideals in one dark body....
>   The history of the American Negro is the history of this
> strife—this longing to attain self-conscious manhood, to
> merge his double self into a better and truer self....He
> would not Africanize America for America has too much
> to teach the world and Africa. He would not bleach the
> Negro soul in a flood of white Americanism, for he knows
> that Negro blood has a message for the world. He simply
> wishes to make it possible for a man to be both a Negro
> and an American, without being cursed and spit
> upon...(August Meier, *Negro Thought in America, 1880-
> 1915* [Ann Arbor: Univ. of Michigan Press, 1963], p. 190).

It is a dualism that is at the heart of the system of race. People
of darker color feel and act like human beings, but they are told
by society that they are not humans on the same level with white
people. Black people especially have been in the storm so long
because they are always caught between their experience of
being human and their experience of being told that they are not
human in white society. This "caughtness" can lead to a tremen-
dously negative self-image of what it means to be classified as
black in this society. It is a long and sad history.

One hundred years ago, white businessmen in the South
decided it was time to redeem the white South by indicating that
its image as racist and backward was incorrect. They decided to
hold an exposition in the growing city of Atlanta in the fall of
1895. It was called the "Atlanta Cotton States and International
Exposition." To dispel racist images, a black speaker was
needed. Booker T. Washington was chosen, and in September
1895, he gave what amounted to a speech of surrender to white
oppression, including these words:

> The wisest among my race understand that the agitation
> of questions of social equality is the extremest folly, and

that progress in the enjoyment of all the privileges that will come to us must be the result of severe and constant struggle, rather than of artificial forcing. No race that has anything to contribute to the markets of the world is long in any degree ostracized. It is important and right that all privileges of the law be ours, but it is vastly more important that we be prepared for the exercise of these privileges. The opportunity to earn a dollar in a factory just now is worth infinitely more than the opportunity to spend a dollar in an opera house (*Booker T. Washington*, ed. Emma Lou Thornbrough [Englewood Cliffs, NJ: Prentice-Hall, 1969], p. 36).

With these words, Washington named the pattern of the system of race—the oppression of people of darker color while continuing to hold those very same people responsible for their oppression. The emphasis is that black people experience discrimination not because of the system of race but because black people are not ready for those rights. When they make themselves ready, when they prove themselves worthy of receiving these rights, then they will receive them. This is a powerful, negative image of what it means to be black, and it continues today. In every age, black people have sought to affirm their humanity over and over again, but the power of the system of race has also caused some black people to accept the lie. Malcolm X expressed this power to promote black self-hatred thirty years ago in his last address before his assassination in 1965:

We hated our heads, we hated the shape of our nose, we wanted one of those dog-like noses, you know; we hated the color of our skin, hated the blood of Africa that was in our veins. And in hating our features and our skin and our blood, why we had to end up hating ourselves. Our color became to us a chain—we felt it was holding us back; our color became to us like a prison which we felt was keeping us confined, not letting us go this way or that way. We felt that all of these restrictions were based solely upon our color, and the psychological reaction to that would have to be that as long as we felt imprisoned or chained or trapped by black skin, black features, and black blood, that skin and those features and that blood holding us back automatically had to become hateful to us. It made us feel inferior; it made us feel inadequate; made us feel helpless (Cone, pp. 290-91).

Would that this process were old and ancient history that has passed on, banished with the civil rights movement! Yet it continues, as we see in these words from a "conservative" black author in 1993:

Even to this day I have a tiny fear that one day I will open a newspaper and find, printed for all the world to see, the story of some nerdy scientist who has uncovered undeniable proof that black people are innately inferior to every other race. I can see the headlines now: "German Scientist Wins Nobel Prize for Genetic Discoveries Proving the Inferior Status of the Black Race." And the lead paragraph will explain that his findings have been confirmed by a team of scientists hand-picked by the NAACP (Spencer Perkins and Chris Rice, *More Than Equals* [Downers Grove, IL: InterVarsity Press, 1993], p. 97).

This process goes on daily in the lives of people of darker color, especially African-American people. They feel and act like human beings, but they must always struggle against the definition given them by the system of race. To be black is to do two things that are especially difficult: to seek affirmation of one's own humanity in a world that denies that humanity and to engage constantly the negative images of oneself.

In this storm, black people can choose from several options; some are chosen by the same individual and kept in delicate balance. The first option is to accept the white definition of being black—bad, lacking, scary, confusing. Those who choose this option usually accept the white lie that this negative image can be overcome by working hard. One of the manifestations of this option is hairstyle. Some African-American men and women go to great lengths to make their hair look "white." This is, of course, a personal choice on one level; but on another level, it is an acceptance of the white definition of physical appearance. The continuing discussion in the black community about light and dark tones of skin color and which is better is another example of the dominance of the white definition. The idea that problems in the African-American community are related to deficiencies in black culture is another manifestation of this negative image. Many African-American people are threatened by their sisters and brothers who are homeless, poor, or convicted of crimes, because they fit the stereotype of the white community and thus threaten their own sense of humanity.

A poignant moment for me as a pastor came a couple of years ago when one of our African-American members came to see me. I consider myself privileged that African-Americans will allow me to be their pastor and thus allow a white man into their lives. Part of the dynamics of life in our multiracial church is that it takes a while for black members to trust me as their pastor. Because I am white and because they have learned to distrust whites, there are barriers to overcome in our pastor-member relationship. A particular member who came to see me was hurt and angry because he had discovered that hard work and a middle-class life-style would not make him acceptable as a human being in a white society. He had thought that if he did great work and was successful, then his skin color would disappear. It had been brought home to him that this was not the case, that skin color would always matter in a white-dominated culture—no matter how much he achieved.

One of the blatant lies created by the system of race is that those called black can gain some measure of humanity by working hard and doing right. There is a genuine danger in which the system of race shifts responsibility for its oppression from the white people, who created it, to those called blacks by it. The system of race thus posits that racism is the result not of the white desire to maintain control, but of the black people's being inferior and less worthy. What seems to be racism is not racism at all—it is the *natural* reaction of white people encountering those less than themselves.

A second option for people of darker color is to withdraw from white people. This can take many forms, from a refusal to let white people into their personal lives to a systematic effort to separate completely. One of our black church members tells me that black people can't be around white people all the time. They must be with their own people on certain occasions so they can be themselves without having to deal with white people. This statement seems ridiculous to many white people, but our reaction comes from our unwillingness and inability to comprehend the daily journeys black people must take through the labyrinth of race.

From Henry McNeal Turner to Marcus Garvey to the Nation of Islam, the desire for separatism has always been part of the dialogue in the black community. This desire for separatism is not racism in reverse, as many white folks like to claim. It is an option born of frustration, anger, pain, and resignation. It is just too much trouble to deal with white people who don't even seem to want to try to understand. Separatism is an idea that grows not out of a desire to say how bad white people are; it is a movement born out of a desire to affirm the humanity of black people. Hear Pearl Cleage's obvious joy in the celebration of her people.

The line was outside, around the block, and it was cold. January in Harlem is always cold. But this was a line of brothers who didn't care. And if they cared, they didn't complain. They waited patiently, some of them talking quietly to other men in line, but more stood silent, waiting for Minister Louis Farrakhan.

There were other brothers there, too, already proudly entering the hall. Members of the Nation of Islam, these brothers wore suits. They arrived in immaculate cars in groups of three and four. Smiling. Dignified. Focused. They nodded to the brothers in line and the brothers in line nodded back with respect.

As the camera panned the line, I realized that I hadn't seen a group of Black men who exuded that level of collective strength, self-confidence and peace in years and I leaned closer to the television, studying their faces, in awe of the spiritual power of Minister Farrakhan to garner the respect of these desperate, disillusioned men who have

learned through experience to suspect everybody, including, maybe especially, each other.

But now, here they were, together. Men who looked like
my father and my uncles and my cousins and my lover
and my daughter's boyfriend were in line with men who
looked like the predators who hang around the crackhouse
down the street and the hard-working mailman who has
to keep one eye out for the neighborhood pit bull and
sweet-faced Simon who comes around to do odd jobs until
he can find something full-time and the man who used to
beat his wife until my True Love showed him a different
way to get along with women.

They were all there, together, drawing strength from
each other in a way that raised such love and hope and
desire in me that I actually caught my breath. Look out, I
thought to myself....That line, wrapping around the Ar-
mory in Harlem tapped into the reservoir of love denied
and dreams deferred that exists in every Black woman I
know and once it kicks in, we are helpless to look away.
The sight of those African-American men, in charge of and
in control of themselves, made me want their presence and
their strength and their love so badly I couldn't stand to
think about it (*Atlanta Tribune,* March 15, 1994, p. 28).

Many black people wonder whether such an affirmation will
ever be acceptable in this society. Indeed, the Nation of Islam is
continually bombarded with charges of racism. Whenever black
people affirm and assert their humanity, white people get nerv-
ous, edgy, and upset. White people seem unable to tolerate the
assertion of the humanity of African-Americans; the tendency
toward separatism remains strong.

As difficult as these first two options are, a third—to engage
white people and white society with dignity—is even more
difficult. It is the most difficult option for black people because
it requires constant vigilance and can elicit both strong rejection
and subtle abuse. It often means being seen as militant by whites
and as selling out by blacks. It often means feeling lost, without
a home, without a haven, seeking to live in a foreign territory.
Yet, it may be the only hope for us—blacks and whites—as a

culture. The engagement of white people by black people—black people who refuse white definitions—may be our only hope to begin to take some baby steps to get us out of the wreckage of the system of race. We who are white are asked to listen to those black people who engage us as fellow human beings. We are asked to see this engagement for what it is—not a threat, but a gift, a flicker of hope and possibility in a crazy and confused world. It is a perilous journey—Dante's trip into Hades and Milkman's journey to find himself in Toni Morrison's *Song of Solomon* demonstrate the perils. It is a difficult and lonely journey, and I want to share the reflections of one black person who is attempting it: Inez Fleming.

Inez Fleming, an African-American elder at Oakhurst Church, is a remarkable person in this culture, remarkable because she is a black person willing to engage white people on our turf. While there are more black people like her that we whites want to acknowledge, it is still a great gift and a great challenge that she brings to those of us who claim the name "white." She engages us as human beings and expects us to act like human beings. I am grateful to her for engaging me and other Oakhurst members, and I am grateful for her contributions to this book and her continuing contributions to the redemptive process of seeking to live as a beloved community.

Inez was elected an elder by our congregation in 1991, and she continues to push us to live out the vision of the beloved community. She has come to her insights and her position through her living and her willingness to engage and to examine her life. She is a single mother, with three grown children (two of whom are members at Oakhurst), and a teen-age daughter (also a member at Oakhurst). As I write, she has just taken in two youths from an Oakhurst family struggling with problems. At her current employment, she continues to see the powerful effects of racism. She works at a cemetery that was previously reserved for burials of white bodies. Now owned by black people, a large part of its business is the removal of bones of what used to be white people by their white families. The white flight never ends—even in death we flee. What will happen when we get to heaven?

I am grateful to her for sharing some of her story. When many of us who are white engage someone like Inez, we feel that she is angry, militant, arrogant, or just plain wrong. We believe that she has been blinded by the power of race. Let us consider that maybe those of us who are white are blinded by the power of race as we hear her reflections on what it means to be black in this society.

• • •

"An Idiot for Fooling with White Folks"

Nibs Stroupe and I do workshops on racism together. These workshops are usually sponsored by liberal white groups who believe that they have made progress on race but who also believe that they need to make more progress. The racial classification of the vast majority of these groups is white. In these workshops, there comes a time when I share what it means to be black in this country. The vast majority of participants in these workshops are usually white; and when I give my interpretation of being black, the white folks almost always react with anger, with defensiveness, and with a sense that they are being unfairly attacked. Some even tell me that I shouldn't be feeling what I am feeling, that there is little race consciousness left in white folks. It is usually a rough-and-tumble session, and I often ask myself why I put myself through this. I don't need it, and the white folks don't want it.

In one particular workshop when the white folks were particularly rowdy, Nibs answered one person with these words: "Instead of attacking Inez, we should be grateful to her for letting white people glimpse her life as a black person. On many levels, she is an idiot for fooling with white folks." Instead of comforting me, his words stung me. Here I was being attacked, and my pastor and my friend was calling me an idiot. So much for pastoral concern!

Yet, as I thought about it later, I decided that he was right. I am an idiot for fooling with white folks. It causes nothing but trouble, and in a world of troubles, who needs more? So, I find my life vacillating between the need for shelter and haven of my people and the call I feel to work against racism. To work against racism means to fool with white folks. And that ain't no fun! They deny my feelings; they are offended by me; they offend me; they deny my humanity. Who needs it?

As strange as it may seem for a person to admit to being an idiot for any reason, I must say that it is true. After asking myself many times, Why am I putting myself through all of this turmoil? the answer has become very clear. I am an idiot for fooling with white folks. As I wonder what to do with these feelings, I recall that St. Paul mentioned the foolishness of God. So, I guess you could say that I am a fool for Christ! I am speaking as a black female. I do not claim to speak for all black people, but I do believe that my story reflects a general sense of what it means to be black in this country.

I am an African-American woman, born and reared in the South prior to and during the civil rights movement. I am also an elder in the multiracial Oakhurst Presbyterian Church in Decatur, Georgia; and my pastor is a white man. It should be no surprise that these two parts of myself have not often fit well together. The whole purpose of the system of race is to make certain that whites and blacks do not get together as equals and as partners. I want to share my story as background and as an endorsement for this book on the enduring power of racism.

I am the seventh child of an African Methodist Episcopal preacher and his wife. I grew up in the port city of Phenix City, Alabama, which is separated from Columbus, Georgia, by the Chattahoochee River.

My childhood was spent going to church in the country every Sunday and interacting with kin folks during the week. We played together, attended school together, and celebrated special occasions together. The extended family was very important in our lives. I can remember spending a lot of quality time with both my paternal and maternal grandparents. Aunts and uncles, great-aunts and great-uncles, and numerous cousins were almost as much a part of my everyday life as my immediate family. I grew up with the knowledge that there were many individuals who loved and nurtured me.

Phenix City is an interesting little city. The racism that existed there was not very visible through my childhood eyes. I can't remember anybody's ever addressing the issue. The childhood memory that sticks with me is that I was constantly told by my people that I was somebody and that I had to be the best that I could be. Being poor and being oppressed by white folks were not acceptable reasons for not succeeding. Expectations were always very high. I was not allowed to accept the white definition of me. The civil rights movement did come to my area, but I watched it from a distance. While a couple of my siblings got involved, it didn't happen for me. I seem to have been protected from a lot of the turbulence associated with the movement, but there are vivid memories that linger; I want to share two of them.

One incident happened one Sunday morning as my family drove to church. A car with about five white persons began to pass us. As they were passing, they began yelling: "Niggers, get off this road! There ain't no place for you niggers!" At the time I was about seven years old, and fear gripped my whole being. I thought that we were going to be killed. I looked at my parents for some sign of reassurance. They just stared straight ahead. No comment, no emotion, nothing. I was terrified. I remember being glad that we were not harmed; but at the same time, I became very fearful of white folks.

The second incident occurred when our back-door neighbor, who was white, told us that we would have to call his granddaughter (our playmate) "Miss Linda" because she had reached her thirteenth birthday. Our reaction was that we did not call her "Miss Linda" or anything else. Her playtime with us was brought to an abrupt end.

I am now a single parent with four children and a granddaughter. Although I had known the sting of racism throughout my life, I really began to feel its oppressive power when I became a single parent. I was forced to seek employment and thus to become involved with "the system," the system of race. I tried to have as few dealings with white folks as possible, but I soon found out that this was impossible. Most avenues led to them; and soon I found myself out in the white world, and I had to learn how "to deal."

"To deal" is the art of encountering white folks on their turf without allowing them to take your humanity. It is a very difficult process, and it was especially hard for me because I had been reared to always be nice. It was, and continues to be, a terrific struggle for me, for there is a great price to be paid whichever way I go—being nice or being honest. Like the prophet Jeremiah, I complained to God about this situation, but I got the same reply that Jeremiah got from God: "You have been racing with slow, country folk—now you will have to race with the swift horses of the city!" Little did I know that this learning "to deal" with white folks was just the beginning.

My first conscious relationship with white folks began in 1982 when I became a sales manager for a major distributor of housewares. The employees at the distributorship were ninety percent white and ten percent black. Little did I know that my experience with this company would give me an education about white folks that would be very instrumental in my understanding of what it means and how it feels to deal with white folks.

When I entered this world and began my sales training, I was full of excitement. This was my first real job, and I was going to prove to myself and to the world how good I was. Reality began to sink in quickly, however. The training I received was in white folks' language and was under the white folks' model. We were told not to work on weekends, but I knew that weekends were prime time for my people. The emphasis on never delivering the product without prior payment misunderstood the cash flow situation of my people. The trainers assumed that black people would follow the white folks' model—they did not understand the vast gap between black and white. When I raised these issues, it was made clear to me that I just didn't understand how a business was really operated.

There were many rules and regulations when it came to the procedures for selling the products and for handling personal accounts by the business office. I kept my eyes and ears open because I know human beings, including white human beings. I knew that there was another informal system that operated alongside the formal system that was being presented to us in the training—and I knew that this informal system was as important, if not more important, than the formal system. I wanted to learn this informal system, but I knew it would be tough to learn it because I was black in a white world.

I deliberately became friendly with the white sales managers because I understood that if I was going to learn how the system really worked and become successful, I would have to fool with the white folks. I would have to absorb a lot of blows, and I did. Because of my personality, I quickly became a favorite with the white folks; and this was unusual in 1982. They began to invite me to outside functions as their guest. Whenever we traveled, they always wanted me as a roommate. All of this acceptance tempted me to believe that I was wonderful, but I knew its real source. The white folks wanted to demonstrate their willingness to accept black folks. They wanted to show me and themselves that they were not racist. I was amazed at the number of white folks who introduced me as their "friend," when I was barely their acquaintance. What a joke! I was their token black center-piece, demonstrating to all the world that they were not racist. They never considered my feelings or me as a person.

This invisibility of my personhood was made painfully clear again and again. When we traveled in a car, back in the days before self-service gas stations were widespread, we would stop for gas at a gas station. If a white attendant came out, the white women would hop out to the bathroom or the soda machines. If a black attendant came out, they would say, "Take your purses and lock the doors," seeming to forget that I was black. They also discussed many other racial matters from a white folks' view in my presence, never hinting at any sensitivity about how I might receive such comments.

When it came to sales, however, they suddenly remembered my blackness. Because I had learned both the formal and the informal systems, I began to be very successful. As my sales mounted, I was promoted and allowed to recruit my people for a sales unit. As our sales mounted and went above the sales of the "white" units, the regional distributors took notice and began to use our record as a motivating device for white folks. In our regional meetings, the white regional distributors would emphasize the high volume of our sales, and they would say to the whites: "You don't want Inez's unit to beat you, do you?" I knew that there was a naturally competitive edge in the sales business, but I also knew that my blackness added a special dimension. The regional managers were really saying: "You white women are not going to let a black woman beat you, are you?"

I had expected these kinds of reactions from white folks because that is the way white folks generally behave around us black folks. As difficult as their behavior was, I was not greatly shocked because I had tried to prepare myself for it. I was less prepared, though, for the reaction of my people in the company. Even though I moved at ease with and was drawn to the black managers, they saw my association with the white saleswomen as something negative. They felt as though I were denying my blackness, as if I were trying to "get white." Quite the contrary. I knew that to serve my people in the business, I would have to gain access to the system. The only way to do it was through the white women. My sisters saw it as a denial of myself and my people. I saw it as a necessity to help myself and my people.

Although I am not now with this company, the painful journey continues for me. To make progress for justice, I must engage white folks as well as my people. When I engage white folks, I am told that I am angry and that I should not raise issues of race. When I engage white folks, my people see me as selling out or they attack me for making white people uncomfortable. I have felt this same process at my church, Oakhurst Presbyterian Church. As has been indicated, we are a multiracial church, but we have our share of problems, too. We are not without the dynamics of race. After all, we have a white male pastor, and I have learned that this is usually the case in these kinds of multiracial churches. But, how many whites would come to a church with a black, male pastor? I'm getting ahead of myself here—let me go back a bit.

Until 1986, I attended and worked hard in the traditional black Methodist church. That year I married an African-American man who was a member of Oakhurst. I came over to Oakhurst with the intention of winning my husband back over to my church, the black church. I could not believe that any self-respecting African-American would be a part of a church with a lot of white folks and especially with a white man as a pastor. The black church was about the only place we could be ourselves without the oppressive presence of white folks. Our church was a refuge for us—we didn't have to be bothered with white folks.

I discovered that Oakhurst was not quite what I thought it was. Oh, there were white folks there who troubled me, to be sure; but there was also a glimmer of hope. There actually seemed to be some white folks there who genuinely wanted to learn about their own racism and about my people. Motives are never pure, but there seemed to be a willingness to listen to us and to our story. I also heard through my involvement at Oakhurst that I didn't always have to be "nice." I heard that to affirm my identity as an African-American was positive. I also heard that it was not only permissible to acknowledge the power of racism in this diverse community of faith—it was an absolute necessity, part of the faith journey.

I began to sense the possibility of a shift in myself, but I was extremely hesitant about getting involved at Oakhurst. It was all new to me—there were white folks there, with a white, male leader. As a black person, all my warning signs went up—proceed with extreme caution. To make yourself vulnerable as a black person to white folks is to put yourself at great risk. I was torn between what I felt was loyalty to my people and an increasing desire to test out this multiracial congregation. In my opinion, you could not put black and white together in any healthy fashion. Yet, Oakhurst did need plenty of help in this area, and I was hearing from the white, male pastor that it could happen with integrity. I could be myself as a black person and not be crushed. So, I decided to try it, amid much protest from my black friends. After all, if I really believed what I had always professed to believe—that *all* persons are brothers and sisters in Christ—then I would need to begin to relate to the white part of the family. Easier said than done!

I felt great frustration at first. I couldn't read the signals of white folks, and I didn't know how to translate them. With the help of the pastor and others, I began to be able to find sources for translation. My biggest concern in becoming involved, however, was not my encounters with white folks at Oakhurst. My biggest concern was how my involvement and views would be received by my people at Oakhurst. The strong position I intended to take as a black person was not part of the picture at Oakhurst at that time. The thoughts I began to share as a black person were not always welcome. Although there were some tense moments because I was raising the issue of race, thanks to God, things began to shift and to fall into place.

There are still tremendous problems at Oakhurst related to "race," but I believe that we have made a start that is real. I recognize that in my lifetime "race" will always be present, but my constant prayer is that we all can work toward that time when we all will be seen first as human beings, as a variety of colors in God's garden. I am now an elder at Oakhurst, on its governing board, and the chairperson of the Christian Education Committee. I traveled to Nicaragua in 1993, and I learned that white folks act the same in other countries as they do here. I also learned in Nicaragua of the indomitable human spirit, which refuses to be crushed by any system. I stay involved at Oakhurst because I continue to be filled with joy when I can say without fear or concern of being shunned: "Say it loud! I'm black, and I'm proud!"

I am often asked by my friends and acquaintances, "Why even bother? Why are you over there devoting your time and talents and energy to white folks? Why not invest all of this in your own people?" I must admit that sometimes I ask myself the same questions: Why do I work with white folks? Why do I feel that working with white folks is so important in the struggle against racism? Am I cheating my own people by spending time and energy on white folks? The answer to me is clear—every person has an obligation to actively participate in seeking to create a better world for succeeding generations. The only way this will happen is for all to address the number one problem in our culture—racism. To address racism means to encounter white folks.

I made the difficult and perilous decision to become involved at Oakhurst, to engage the white folks there. It has been a roller-coaster ride, with feelings of accomplishment and feelings of idiocy. I have experienced difficult encounters with white folks and with my people at Oakhurst. As it was in the business world, so it is with the church. I *expect* difficulties with white folks, but I am disappointed with difficulties with my folks.

I am not certain that any good has come from these encounters, but at least I have learned that the system of race has the power to tear apart my people. Race is a monster, and all of us who are black must face it. Indeed, I prefer the name "black" to "African-American" because I take the white folks' negative image of me and stand up to them: "Say it loud—I'm black and proud." To say that "black is beautiful" is not to misunderstand or misuse the language. It is to comprehend it only too well and to challenge it on its own terms. No begging to be recognized as a human being, no seeking to please the white folks. Just to be. And to be proud of that being, whatever white folks may decide to call it.

I have not always been as strong in my sense of blackness. While I was always proud to be black, I also had difficult times in dealing with my blackness. There was a period in my life when I had accepted some of the white definition of being black. I came to believe that if my people had problems, the only reason for the problems was that something was wrong with us and that race had nothing to do with it at all. Even though I knew the power of race, I felt that we should have bettered ourselves, that if we worked hard enough, we would succeed.

I have since learned better. I have relearned the system of race, this time from both an analytical and an experiential perspective. My people and I still have a lot to learn. Many of us have fallen into the trap of materialism. We believe that we can prove our self-worth by the material things we acquire. Many of us believe that if we could just get properly educated and get a good job, we would be accepted by whites. This is a white lie, a devious diversion from the system of race. Although white folk want us to believe this lie, the truth is that white folks do not intend to accept us as human beings and do not intend to share power with us. This truth is a given in the system of race, and it should never be forgotten. Never.

I have encountered these struggles at Oakhurst among my people. When I assert my identity as a black woman at Oakhurst, my own people tell me that I am too negative or that I am antiwhite. Once, a sister introduced me as a black racist to a visitor at the church. A discussion in our church's governing body was particularly difficult for me. I am an elder, which is an elected position, and part of that governing body. The committee that I chair as elder recommended to the governing body, the Session, that we endorse the formation of a black women's group in our church. Nibs and I anticipated trouble on this recommendation, and we tried to prepare for it. But, we were not prepared for it; indeed, I don't know that I could ever have been prepared for it.

The problem that we encountered on this question at Oakhurst was our own self-image. We are a multiracial church, and part of our image as Oakhurst is a wonderful community where everyone gets along. The reality is something different, however. Please don't misunderstand me. Oakhurst is a significant and powerful community of faith because it has dared to try to tell and to live the truth that the Gospel is more important than race. It is a place unlike most places in this society. If I did not think that it was significant and that it offered possibilities, I would not be at Oakhurst.

Like all approaches to race, however, we at Oakhurst, too, want to move quickly over race without really encountering it, "we" meaning both black and white. So, when the recommendation was made to start a black women's group in a place that was supposed to be beyond race, it struck a lot of hearts. One sister made a strong point: If a white woman had come with a recommendation to start a white women's group, we would turn it down without discussion. So, why should we promote a group that seems to oppose what Oakhurst believes? A brother made the point that we were emphasizing race too much at Oakhurst and that this recommendation was evidence of that. One white woman commented that while she could see a need for such a group, an endorsement by us would be the same as endorsing the system of race.

Another sister supported the recommendation, saying that she felt the need for this group. She felt that many black women at Oakhurst faced immense problems from their own particular histories and from the culture at large, and that they needed a place to share them and to seek solutions. She also said that we were not being realistic if we felt that the group would be the same if white women came. The sharing would simply not be the same because black women were not accustomed to sharing their lives with white folks, to do so was to invite destruction.

During this discussion, Nibs, my pastor and friend, disappointed me. He moderated the meeting; and while he gave verbal support to the proposal, I noticed a shift in the discussion as he led us through it. I don't know whether it was caused by his whiteness or his desire to avoid a split in the governing body, since the discussion indicated a close vote. He began to steer us toward a compromise in which the Session would allow the group to meet in our building but would not formally endorse it. Most of the elders seemed agreeable to this until it came to me. I would not accept it. At this point, Nibs became conscious of what he had done; and I do appreciate that he then publicly stated that with his input he had steered us away from the original motion and toward the compromise. He apologized. White people never cease to amaze me!

The motion to endorse a black women's group was back before us. Then the real turning point came; for me it was both good news and bad news. A white sister spoke in support of the proposal, saying that she understood the objections and the seeming contradiction but felt that we ought to listen to the reality. The real question was not how it would appear but whether we wanted to assist black women in our congregation. If we wanted to help them deal with the power of race that sought to crush their lives both individually and communally, then we ought to try to respond in this manner. From my point of view, her comments were crucial because of the timing and because she was white. The motion passed by a close vote of 5-4. The vote crossed racial lines—three blacks and two whites for it and two blacks and two whites against it. One brother abstained, and the pastor didn't vote.

Why did I say the white sister's comments were both good news and bad news? Why have I gone into such detail about this decision? The reason is that this discussion is central to my struggles as a black woman in engaging the system of race and because it tells so much about what is really going on. My white sister's comments were good news because it was clear that she was listening and that she was understanding. It can happen—white people can hear us and listen to us. I know that her own personal history had helped her develop sensitivity, but I also like to think that her being a part of Oakhurst helped to develop her sensitivity. She even called me later to tell me that she appreciated my persistence and that she had some sense of the difficulty of the process for me. And it was good news because I do believe that her comments came at a crucial time.

It was bad news to me because the crucial comments came from a white person. I am not saying that the earlier comments by the sister in favor of the proposal were not crucial. They were crucial because it affirmed that it was not just "bad" Inez's proposal. Yet, I cannot help but feel that the favorable comments from a white person tipped the scale in favor of the motion.

This decision was important to me because, although it went the way I felt it should go, it has reinforced my sense that in multiracial settings such as Oakhurst, my sisters and brothers get uncomfortable when someone like me comes along to raise issues of race. It is as if we are still in the mode of making white people feel comfortable, just as we've always been. If the white pastor raises the issue, that is irritating but acceptable because he is white and the pastor. If a black sister raises the issue, she must be punished for getting out of her place and making both whites and blacks uncomfortable. In an all-black church, this recommendation about a black women's group would need no discussion. And people wonder why some of us tend toward "separatism"!

What does it mean to be black? It means to be in the storm—to be constantly criticized for rocking the boat. It is painful and angering and frustrating. I have many unanswered questions: Should I spend so much time with white folks, trying to get them to understand black folks, trying to get them to understand the power of racism? Is it right to take my energy and use it in what I feel is sometimes an impossible mission? Am I cheating my own people by not giving them one hundred percent? These and many other questions haunt me as I encounter the system of race. Perhaps what haunts me the most, however, is that I don't know if I'll ever find the answers. Yet, I know I must try. And, I have crossed the line now. Here I am at Oakhurst.

What does it mean to be black? It means to seek to weather the storm of racism. And yet, it also means to celebrate. I believe that this is what irritates white folks the most—in the midst of the battering storm, we still dance and sing and celebrate! We will not finally be defined by race or by white folks. We will be defined by that African heritage that still has not been beaten out of us, even after four hundred years of oppression. Why do we play our music so loud? To let everybody know, black and white, that we are alive and full of life. To let everybody know that, despite our problems and the oppression, we are a people who know life's true meaning. Why do we celebrate our bodies? Because we believe in the incarnation, that God came among us in the flesh, to lift us all up as a mystery of spirit and flesh. Because we know it is our bodies that have been the focal point of racism—from workhorse in the fields to steel-drivin' men to the flesh of our sisters. We mourn the loss of our bodies to white folks, but we celebrate our bodies as affirmation that we do not finally belong to the system of race.

What it means to be black, then, is to encounter an incredible amount of pain and negativity. What it means to be black, then, is to be in a battle for our lives and to find a way to survive when no way seems possible. What it means to be black, then, is to find a resource of power and meaning and celebration that remains invincible to racism. What it means to be black, then, is to find our true definition as children of the God who rules over all. It is that definition that will sustain us and that definition we celebrate as we blare out our music and laugh so loud. We are black. We are proud.

Nancy Anne Dawe

The Semitic (dark skinned) Jesus

Nancy Anne Dawe

Members of Oakhurst Presbyterian Church

Nancy Anne Dawe

Time for the children during worship

Nancy Anne Dawe

The Sanctuary Mass Choir

Nibs Stroupe

A baptism, 1992

Nibs Stroupe

Community fair, 1992, a Nigerian potter, a member of
Oakhurst, demonstrates his skills

The Christmas pagent, 1993

Nibs Stroupe

Closing of worship with the congregation circling the sanctuary singing "Sweet, Sweet Spirit"

Nancy Anne Dawe

CHAPTER 6

"Seeing in a Mirror Dimly"— What It Means to Be White

I am a white, male Southerner. I carry the baggage of all three of those categories, and others as well. As a Southerner, I know firsthand the power of racial classification. My white Southern forebears have been the most recent of American culture to openly affirm their racial identity as white people. I have benefited from it, and I have also claimed the name white.

There are numerous studies, novels, and essays on the topic of what it means to be black in this country, yet little has been written on what it means to be white. On one level, that may seem surprising; but a bit of reflection will demonstrate why there is such a paucity of writing on the meaning of "whiteness." In this society, to be white is to be normal, and so the meaning of being white is clear—a regular human being struggling and celebrating in life. It is the abnormal ones whom we must study, especially those we call black. Why are they so different? Why are they so foreboding and threatening? We say that they are the ones who need analysis, not us.

There is no need to study whiteness because that is the essence of humanity itself. This sense of normality or the goodness of being white is one of the results of the system of race, and we must now take a careful look at what it means to be white to discern the inner workings of this system. It may seem, as St. Paul stated, that we are looking in a mirror dimly as we search for what it means to be white; but we must search for that image as accurately as we can. It is elusive but it is central to our identity, and to confronting the power of race in our time.

A bit of review is in order. One's racial classification is fundamental in this culture—more important, it seems, than class, gender, or sexual orientation. This is not to seek to diminish the importance of those categories but rather to acknowledge how central racial classification is in our society. The great and yet disturbing irony about this classification is that it is not based on biology or science or genetics. Race is a political and social construct, designed to determine who will have access to power and who will not. This is especially true of the category of white, which encompasses many people—Italians, Swedes, Russians, French, English, and so on. It has not always been this way. In the past, Irish, Italians, Turks, and many others have had a difficult time breaking into the category, although they have done so in the end. We are less certain about people of Latino origin and even more uneasy about people from the Middle East. And Jewish people? They have had the most difficult time of all, sometimes being seen as a race of their own, sometimes being seen as white.

Indeed, part of the source of the continuing tensions between Jewish people and African-American people is the fluidity of being white. Jewish people have been oppressed and persecuted, and they continue to face discrimination. In this sense, they understand the power of racism. Yet, they are able to cross over; they at times are seen as part of the white race; they sometimes see themselves as white, and African-Americans see them as white. When a Jewish person claims that Jews, too, know persecution by whites, the African-American response is often scorn, a reply born of a sense that African-Americans can never cross over to be seen as white or acceptable. When African-Americans claim that Jewish people are part of the white conspiracy to eradicate people of darker color, the Jewish response is that Jewish people are not white and have indeed known persecution by whites.

Whiteness, then, is arbitrary and fluid; and yet it is fundamental. To be white is to have doors opened that are closed to others. To be white is to have a sense of being a standard for humanity. To be white is to have access to opportunity and possibility. To be white is to be human. With this in mind, I want to explore the meaning of what it means to be white through a journey into my own history.

My grandfather's grandfather owned people. I do not know if he saw them as people. I know that he saw them as slaves. Contrary to some historical interpretations of slavery, it was not just the wealthy planter class that used slave labor. It was dirt farmers, yeoman farmers like my great-great grandfather. To say that my family owned people called slaves is not to say that I am overwhelmed with guilt. It is to say that as a person who has been given the name white, and accepted the name white, I must always keep my family history in front of me, because it offers a clue to the nature of racism.

As far as I can ascertain, my familial ancestors were decent people. They were not the stereotype of racists, lynching black people or terrorizing the countryside in white sheets at night. As far as I can discern, my forebears were good and decent people—they loved the earth, they loved one another, they offered hospitality to strangers, and they had a good sense of humor. They were good people, and they helped to nurture me and my understanding of the world and gave me great gifts.

And they were racists. That sounds harsh, doesn't it? It is difficult for me to write, even at this moment. My grandfather, with his great belly laugh and overly generous heart, my grandfather who cuddled me and told me that I was his favorite (as I'm sure he told all his grandchildren!), my grandfather was a racist. It is difficult to acknowledge that such a loving and kind man was a racist. And yet, it is true.

It is this juxtaposition of being decent and yet participating in evil that is important to keep before us. If we lose sight of this juxtaposition, we lose sight of one of the central dynamics of the system of race. Often, we deny racism in white people by believing that the only racists are the brutish louts who enjoy stomping and crushing black people. It is much deeper and much more complex than that. I know. I have it in my family history and in my own consciousness. I want to keep my family history before me not because I am worried about my ancestors and filled with guilt but because I must worry about what I am doing and what my children are doing in relation to the system of race. My family history instructs me that good and decent white people can be racists.

I was born in 1946 in Memphis, Tennessee, a town that was a focal point of Mississippi Delta culture, a city where cotton was brought from the fields to be sold and shipped on the Mississippi River all over the world. I grew up in Helena, Arkansas, a farming town on the Mississippi River that is much more like the Mississippi Delta culture than the other parts of Arkansas. I cannot remember a time when I did not know race. There were whites and there were "niggers" and there were others who didn't quite fit in either category: Chinese, Jews, Italians, Mexicans. These latter people were lumped into the category of white, but they were not quite like us, yet they were different from black people.

To call a black person a "nigger" was not a pejorative term to me. It was more a given, a natural name, like "dog" or "cat" or "house." I don't even remember sensing that in using the word "nigger," I was drawing a line to mark the great divide. It was simply what and who black people were. Yet, as a white Southerner, I was ever aware of the foreboding otherness of black people. There was something mysterious and dark and forbidden about them. There was the knowledge, not brought to consciousness, but rather deep in my soul, of the troubling presence of dark-skinned people.

Indeed, even though they lived only a few houses away from me in my childhood years, I had no awareness that those I called "niggers" were people like me. Though my family was relatively poor, we shared leftover food and used clothing with a black family that lived down the street. In these encounters, the closest I had, since I went to segregated schools, I had no idea who these creatures really were, but it was clear to me that they were not like me. And it was clear that it was forbidden and dangerous to explore who they really were. I sometimes had a sense as a boy that there was more to it than I had been taught. I remember thinking, What if they really are like us? Such exploration was dangerous and forbidden because it could lead to a difficult truth: They are like us; they are human beings just like me. But I was only a boy, and a fatherless boy at that. I was not about to take on such a dangerous exploration when I was so unsure of my own manhood and worthiness.

That was long ago and far away, however, and a lot has changed. "Nigger" is no longer an acceptable word for whites to use in public discourse. Laws have been passed, schools have been integrated, African-American people have entered areas that no one thought possible. Perhaps I shouldn't try to bring up ancient history, a dialogue inspired by my guilt as a white Southerner. Or have things really changed that much? Listen to a more recent voice from February 1992 (not 1952). Frederick K. Goodwin, head of the Federal Alcohol, Drug Abuse and Mental Health Administration, made these remarks in a public address about a "new research focus on early identification of youths who might become dangerously antisocial."

> If you look, for example, at male monkeys, especially in the wild, roughly half of them survive to adulthood. The other half die by violence. That is the natural way of it for males, to knock each other off and, in fact, there are some interesting evolutionary implications of that because the same hyperaggressive monkeys who kill each other are also hypersexual, so they copulate more and therefore they reproduce more to offset the fact that half of them are dying.
>
> Now, one could say that if some of the loss of social structure in this society, and particularly within the high-impact inner-city areas, has removed some of the civilizing evolutionary things that we have built up and that maybe it wasn't just the careless use of the word when people call certain areas of certain cities jungles, that we may have gone back to what might be more natural, without all of the social controls that we have imposed upon ourselves as a civilization over thousands of years in our own evolution (Chicago *Tribune,* March 21, 1992).

Some people walked out on Goodwin's address, and the furor it created forced him to resign his post. However, Goodwin had made the essential connections in his speech in seeking to maintain the power of the system of race, with the image of inner-city male youths (black) acting like monkeys in the jungle, with this behavior being the natural order of things. Goodwin's speech would be depressing enough if it had been given at a Ku Klux Klan rally; that it was given by a high-level official in the federal government is cause for great alarm. There were two other alarming factors. First, Goodwin claimed that he had no idea that his speech would offend people. Second, while he was forced to resign his post, he was not forced out of government service by his African-American boss, Louis Sullivan. Instead, he was appointed head of the National Institute of Mental Health.

The second incident is a reminder of the terror that has traditionally been used to keep black males under control. On March 6, 1992, a state district judge in Texas accepted a plea bargain to castrate a black man rather than send him to prison for repeated sexual offenses (*Atlanta Constitution,* March 7, 1992). That plea bargain was later rescinded because of the public outcry. It is a sign of hope in both these cases that some shame was lifted up in public. It is a sign of danger that these were initiated not by the "far-right loonies" but by public officials. Whether it is liberals wringing their hands over the continuing major problems for black people or Willie Horton being used to win white votes or public officials treating black males as subhuman, the dangerous signs are with us: White people are reasserting the power of the system of race by attacking the humanity of black people and black culture.

It is not so long ago or far away. Whether we say "nigger" or not, the power of race remains with us as long as we claim the name white. To be white is to see all others as less than we are, as a different species, as those closer to monkeys in the jungle than to us as white people. We may cringe when we hear the comparison to monkeys, but we must realize that if we claim the name white, we are accepting a system that depends on and asserts this comparison.

This is difficult to hear for those of us who are white. Most of us do not say "nigger" in public, and many of us are angered to hear the comparison of black people to monkeys. We consider ourselves above those kinds of actions. To convict us of accepting the entire system of race just because we call ourselves white seems ludicrous. It seems to leave us feeling hopeless and with-out recourse. We can't be "not white." We can't give up our whiteness—it is a given. Are we bad people then? Racists with-out hope? To make the equation white = racist seems to put us in a hopeless and impossible situation. But we must remember, as with me and my family history, that it is possible to be a good and decent person and yet participate in racism.

Again, this juxtaposition of being good *and* participating in evil is important. I want to explore it from another angle, using part of my own history. My father abandoned my mother and me when I was a baby. I never saw him again until I was in my early twenties. Part of my journey as a youth was a struggle with this situation. I wondered why my father never came to see me and why he never contacted me. I concluded that something must be wrong with me. In the midst of my struggle as a youth, the Presbyterian church members in my hometown sought to fill the vacuum. They spent time with me, nurtured me, told me that I was special. It was a great gift; it was what the church is supposed to be. Even now I feel a warmth about the gifts of those church people; and whenever I wonder about whether the church has sold its soul to the culture, I remember this gift. That church mediated God's love to me powerfully and profoundly. As my inner voice told me that I was not worth much because I had no father, their voices told me that I had great worth because they loved me and God loved me. The members of my church were loving, caring, and supportive of me. They were also influential people in the town who helped determine political and social policy: bankers, teachers, planters, and farmers.

And they were racists. Some were more tolerant than others, but they all felt that whites should be in control. They were extremely uncomfortable when the civil rights movement came to the South. They felt that things should stay the same, that political and economic and social power should stay under white control. Few, if any, even considered the idea that the black people, who made up the majority of people in our county, were human beings like them. Black people should not have access to power because they could not handle power. These good and loving people who saw such potential in me and worked to develop that potential could not see the same potential in black people. Their blinders to the humanity of black people did not negate their goodness, but it did make them racists.

This paradox of being good and also being racist is central to being white. We who claim the name white often deny that we participate in racism. When our participation in racism is asserted or even demonstrated, we become defensive and angry. We understand that to participate in racism is somehow to lose our goodness. Despite our struggles to recognize the humanity of black people, we are often unaware of our complicity and participation in racism. When it is revealed, we react in anger or denial or deep sadness. To retain the idea of being good or decent, we must deny that we participate in racism. We experienced this last year when some of the African-American members of our church observed the jury selection and trial of a 13-year-old black boy charged as an adult for armed robbery. When we expressed our concern in a letter to the county district attorney that the boy's race was a significant factor in the decision to try him as an adult, we received a blistering reply on March 31, 1994, from J. Tom Morgan, the district attorney, in which he asserted his freedom from any racism. "I am confident that any member of my church would be shocked if anyone, particularly a Presbyterian minister, would accuse me of making a decision on race." It is only too clear what we are thinking when we assert that we as white people make no decisions based on race.

On this point, I want to return briefly to the issue of intent versus results in relation to racism. I believe that most white people would claim they do not intend to discriminate against people of darker color. The district attorney who was so hurt because we accused him of racism certainly did assert that racism did not guide his decisions. I also believe that many white people do not consciously intend to discriminate against people of darker color. However, the issue of racism cannot be settled only by examining intentions. Since Reconstruction, it has been rare for white people to publicly proclaim that they intend to discriminate based on race. Even the bedrock segregationists of the South cited science and biology, not racism, as reasons for segregation.

To discuss the issue of racism, we must also look at *results*. Do whites who *profess* a lack of racism live in all-white or vast-ma-jority-white neighborhoods? If so, why? Do their children go to all-white or vast-majority-white schools? If so, why? Do they attend an all-white or almost-white synagogue or church? If so, why? Are the vast majority of their friends white? If so, why? If we look at results, an amazing and overwhelming majority of white people who profess a lack of racism demonstrate a pro-found desire to stay out of the presence of people of darker color and stay in the presence of white people. What is the matter with this? Can't we associate with whomever we want to associate? This is not in dispute. What is in dispute is why whites who profess no racism almost always choose to disassociate them-selves from people of other races. If this is not racism—judging people and our association with them according to racial classi-fication—what is it? It is the desire to be "good" and "decent" and "white" at the same time.

The insistence on being able to deny racism while retaining the privileges of being white in the system of race was born in the heart of Southern white religion. Just as white individuals want to maintain this dualism, so it is with our institutions—re-ligion, schools, banking, politics. It was born in the white South-ern religious response to slavery. How could we worship God and still own people called slaves? By denial. By denying that black people were people like us and by denying that God cared about justice. In seeking to come to terms with slavery, God became privatized in the Southern white religious experience as a God who cared only for the salvation of individual souls. We debated at times whether those we called slaves had souls; and when we agreed that they did have souls, we still believed that what was important was the eternal salvation of those souls and not their freedom from slavery. After all, the Bible permitted slavery—St. Paul told the slaves to obey their masters.

We make God subject to individual experience and whims. The God of the prophets, the God who freed the Israelites from slavery in Egypt, this biblical God disappears from the white mind as we seek to limit God to individual salvation. We white Southerners defended racism, and we undergirded the indi-vidualism that was already developing in American culture with an astonishing but pervasive assertion: God cares much more about the salvation of individuals than about justice.

To be white, then, is to participate in racism. The system of race is arbitrary and fluid, and yet, it remains so powerful and so important. Are we damned, then, forever? Are we trapped in whiteness, never to find release or relief? If being white is so awful, how do we come to awareness? Are we so deeply mired in racism that there is no hope? Can we change?

We can change. Some of us are already struggling with change. Over the next two chapters, we will look at the possibilities of change for those of us who are white. For now, however, I want to share some more of my own history to demonstrate that there are possibilities for change, even in what seems to be the most difficult place of all, my white Southern culture.

I want to share some more of my history of coming to awareness about what it means to be white. I have changed and am struggling with my own racism, yet I know that I never will be cured of racism. It is deeply imbedded in my being, and I benefit greatly from my racial classification as white. Those are parts of me that I am desperate to deny. Just as I cringed earlier when I wrote that my wonderful grandfather was a racist, so now I cringe when I say that I am a racist. I do not have a martyr complex, and I am not overwhelmed with guilt. I simply want to acknowledge the continuing power of race in our culture. What is asked of those of us who are called white is not purity or even complete healing—what is asked of us is awareness and acknowledgment.

Just as my family participated in racism, it also sought freedom from it. I experienced this struggle most clearly in my mother. She is a Southern white woman who shares the traits of those categories. In the midst of her participation in racism, she sought to emphasize the humanity of all people. She would not allow me to call black people by their first names. I also remember one particular episode that related to Jewish people. I don't remember how old I was, but I came home from school with a searing hatred of Jews. When my mother came home from work, I told her, "I hate Jews." She asked me why I would say that, and I told her that I hated them just because they were Jews. She replied, "But you don't hate Raymond, do you?" I said, "No, I like Raymond. He's one of my best friends." "What about David?" she asked. "Oh yes, I like him. He's great." "What about Ruth?" "Oh, well, she's a girl, but she's nice." Then my mother summed it up: "Nibs, all of them are Jewish. Do you hate them?" I was shocked. "No, Mother, I don't hate them." My mother drove it home: "Well, Nibs, I think you had better be careful about whom you think you hate." The world was confusing, but I began to think that I had better take more care about what I thought and about what I told my mother!

Although she participated in racism, my mother seemed determined to help me think about it critically. Again and again, she refused to allow me to accept without question the system of race. The seeds of awareness were planted in me by my family in this small Delta town.

A second source of my awareness was my church. I have already indicated its gifts to me. Its members nurtured me and loved me. Despite their participation in racism, their love helped me believe in God and the power of the Gospel. They lived and demonstrated God's love in relationship to me and many others. They mediated God to me, and they planted the seeds of awareness in my life: the call to serve God is first and foremost. The love that my church shared helped me understand that God is alive, that the Gospel can be put into action, and that the Gospel's view of life takes precedence over the world's view of life. When the time came to make a decision on race, I could consider the possibility that God wanted something different than a white world view, even if it meant conflict with those very church members who had nurtured this process in me.

Decision time did come. The civil rights movement in the South was occurring while I was in high school. I attended segregated schools; public school "integration" came much later in my town. I generally reflected the white interpretation of the civil rights movement. I recall bragging with other white boys about going over the Mississippi River bridge at Helena to Oxford, Mississippi, some sixty miles away, to protect the University of Mississippi from the "invasion" of James Meredith in the fall of 1962. As fate would have it, I did go to Ole Miss the next summer to a summer science camp, and I remember feeling uneasy about the passion of white students as they showed me the bullet holes in the campus buildings that were a result of the white riot in response to Meredith's desire to enroll at his state university.

Thus, in high school I was not marching for civil rights; indeed, I was repeating the white response about "communists" and "outside agitators." And yet, there was a feeling growing in me, an uneasiness with the white response, a sense that there might be something valid about the claims of the civil rights movement. The assertion by black people that they were human beings with a dignity equal to that of white people irritated me but struck something deep in me. It was an assertion that called out a struggle and a journey that would change my life.

In Helena one January night in 1966, my childhood friend David Billings and I were discussing our future at a local restaurant. We had both done manual labor the summer before, and as we approached the summer after our sophomore year at college, we were looking for something new, something less physically strenuous! As we threw out various options, I said that I had heard of a church in Brooklyn that hired college students for its summer work in Bedford-Stuyvesant. David's aunt, Peggy Billings, lived in New York, and he had felt the same pull about the civil rights movement as I had. We agreed that I would investigate the possibilities and get back in touch with him. In the meantime, the small-town Southern white boys dreamed of the glamour and possibilities of New York City!

We were accepted as members of the church's summer program staff; it was an experience that changed our lives. For the first time in our lives, we worked with black people as peers, and our supervisors were black people. As Southern white boys, we experienced the gift of a moment when those we had seen as "other" became people and our leaders. Our understanding of the world was altered forever. We were in the presence of African-Americans as people, as human beings like us. There were major differences, to be sure, but for the first time, we experienced the humanity of black people. David and I would never be the same again. He has continued to be a friend, and he has continued to grow and push me to grow in his vocation as a trainer in antiracism work for the People's Institute for Survival in New Orleans.

When I came back to the South after my experience in Brooklyn, I saw life differently. At first I considered that the black people whom I had encountered in Brooklyn were qualitatively different from the black people in my hometown in the South. I still wanted to hold onto my white opinions that I had held so long, but my eyes had been opened, and those opinions could no longer hold me. A shift had taken place—the world did not look the same. I began to feel that the humanity I had experienced in Brooklyn was the same as that in Helena and in Memphis. I could not go back to my former consciousness. The journey had begun.

When I returned at the end of the summer, I shared with my church the excitement of what had been revealed to me. Instead of being met with the enthusiasm I had expected, I was received with silence and stern resistance. The reaction was that I had gone up North and had been perverted—an old story for white Southerners. My soul was in turmoil because the church, one of my parenting figures, rejected both the power and the accuracy of my revelatory experience. This rejection opened a deep chasm in my heart.

I went back to college in Memphis in the fall, and I tried my new approach. I sought to get acquainted with some of the few black students at the school. This process was painful because my assumptions and prejudices about black people were so transparent. When I went into their homes, I was astonished that their houses were very similar to mine. (Lest my reactions seem outmoded and antiquated in the '90s, please note that Andrew Hacker reports studies indicating that more than 80 percent of all white people still have never been in the home of a black person.) What had I expected? I am not certain of what I thought I would encounter, but my surprise came from the assumption that these beings were not creatures like me. This kind of encounter happened again and again, and often the black students perceived my surprise. Some of them were harsh in response to my display of racism, but most were gentle and challenging. The more they let me in their lives, and the more I let them into mine, the more embarrassed I was; yet I felt a profound gratitude that perhaps I was on the right track. What I began to learn in this process was twofold: the stunning depth of my racism with its belief in a vast difference between the humanity of white people and the being of black people and my desire to continue in this process despite the immense distance that I would obviously have to travel. It was clear that I was in unchartered territory—a Southern white boy trying to imagine and live the revolutionary idea that blacks were people just like me.

This process was not occurring in a vacuum, centered only on my personal journey. In the fall, I worked in the political campaign of the first black candidate to run for mayor of Memphis. I learned from that work that some of my white friends felt I was becoming one of the most radical people on campus. The evidence for that conclusion was that I was participating in the rather conventional process of a political campaign. The radical nature came from the fact that the candidate was black. The labeling of my activities helped open my eyes to the depth of the racism around me.

I was not the only white crusader for justice, however. In that same school year, one of my black friends from college was denied entrance into a local restaurant near the campus. We immediately launched a demonstration and boycott of the restaurant. Although many white students castigated our actions, I was pleasantly surprised by the supportive reactions of other white students. We actually had a good turnout; we got the local media interested; the Justice Department began an investigation—and then the restaurant closed down. It was a whirlwind process, and I had many mixed feelings. We had forced someone out of business. Was it worth that? Had we intended that? No, we had intended to affirm the dignity of all people and to affirm their right to have access to public places. We had accomplished some of our goal, but I had also learned first-hand the difference between intentions and results.

In 1968, I worked in support of the garbage workers' strike in Memphis. It was a time of great possibility and great confusion. The year seemed pregnant with the opportunity for progress, despite the great resistance that we encountered. Little did I know that by the end of the year the prophet who had helped to ignite the civil rights movement would be assassinated, that a major presidential candidate would be killed two months later, and that Richard Nixon would be president of the United States. I can remember the moment when I discerned that the confusion was overpowering the possibility. I was coming out of the college library a little after 6:00 P.M. on April 4 when one of the black students came up to tell me that Martin Luther King, Jr., had been shot across town. All kinds of feelings raced across my heart—anger that this had happened, hope that King was still alive, fear for the future. My black friend was ready to fight—indeed, the rage had begun to be expressed in cities all over the country. Dr. King was already dead.

The National Guard and the United States Army poured into Memphis. Instead of the sounds of spring blooming in the city, we heard the sounds of tanks, half-tracks, and gunfire on the streets. Instead of the possibility of reform and renewal, we were all plunged back into confusion where no one was to be trusted. As I have indicated earlier, 1968 was a pivotal year for the civil rights movement, both in society and in our hearts. By the end of that year, the forces of racism had begun to regather their strength. That strength has yet to ebb.

In many ways, most of us who passed through those tumultuous years have lived our lives in reaction to them. For some of us, it meant the end of a vision and a return to the ways of the world. As a former activist friend of mine told me, "The freedom fighters of the '60s have become the gourmet cooks of the '80s." For some of us, it meant a time of questioning and wandering, trying to find our place in a world we felt was deeply unjust but obviously was not going to be immediately transformed by our efforts.

So it has been with me. I graduated from college in 1968 and went on to divinity school. It took me seven years to get through seminary, as I bounced around trying to find my place. On the one hand, I was deeply tied to the church because of its history of transmitting God's love to me. On the other hand, I felt strong anger at the church because it seemed so tied to the culture, especially to racism. I became an ordained pastor, married a pastor, and we shared a church in Norfolk, Virginia. From there to Nashville and to Atlanta, the struggle remained the same:

How could I put these two pieces together? How could I affirm both the church and efforts to fight racism?

Coming to Oakhurst Presbyterian Church, I found that God gave me a glimpse of the answer. This church was a struggling congregation with a gargantuan building and only a few members, but it had taken a huge step from my point of view. It had both black and white members. The great divide in our society that seems to be at its strongest in the institutional church had already been bridged a bit. The deteriorating building, the fortress mentality, and the tenacious hold on power of the white members—all of these daunting factors could not stop my sense that I might be coming home. We came to Oakhurst, and we have had and continue to have many battles; but we have stayed. Here, race and religion can come together, rather than being torn asunder as in the majority of our culture. The struggles remain, but it feels like home.

The journey continues. It has taken me through many places, but I am led to be a witness for justice and to be a witness about racism. It is a journey that will not end any time soon, if at all, even if I want it to end. I want to be able to say, "I am not a racist." I want to be able to truly believe that I see people as people, but I still see black people and white people, Hispanic people and Asian people. That is the power of the system of race. Race and color first—then perhaps humanity next, but more likely no humanity, just racial categories.

In my more lucid moments, I seek to be aware of my racism. It was brought home to me in two recent incidents. In one, Inez Fleming and I were working with some leaders in a justice movement with a long history. We were asked to consult with them because of some racial tensions in this particular justice movement. Inez asked one of the white leaders if he was a racist. He replied, "Well, yes, I guess I am sometimes." I felt for my white brother. He had been laid bare in his racism, but still he had trouble admitting it. He could not bring himself to say that he was a racist because such an admission would mean that his goodness, his decency, and his life's work for justice could be called into question. He was caught in the dilemma of being white, benefiting from and using the system of race but unable to acknowledge it. What he was admitting to Inez was that sometimes he was caught using racism, rather than admitting his racism. She reminded him that being a racist "sometimes" is like being almost pregnant—it is simply not possible.

As I sympathized with my white brother, I remembered a second incident that had happened only a few days before our meeting. I was waiting for the MARTA train to take me to downtown Atlanta. Just as I got on the train, some adolescent black boys got in the same car, cussing and hollering. I sat down in a seat, somewhat on edge from the belligerence of the African-American boys. As the train pulled out from the station, I became aware of a strong smell of alcohol coming from someone sitting behind me. I was curious about it, but I did not want to turn around and look because I didn't want to start any problems. I knew without looking that the smelly passenger was a black man, and I began to think that it was so sad for black men to dissipate their lives in alcohol and drugs. I thought about this as the train pulled in to the next station. The man behind me got up to leave the train. I looked up, and there he was, a well-dressed white man smelling of alcohol. My reaction was not so much shock as a sad irony. The system of race continues to pull at me. I know what it means to be white. The meaning of being white is to deny the power of racism, to believe that we have left it behind. The hope of being white is to allow ourselves to come to awareness and acknowledge the power of race.

CHAPTER 7

"Come to the Waters"

"Later he saw Jesus move from tree to tree in the back of his mind, a wild ragged figure motioning him to turn around and come off into the dark where he was not sure of his footing, where he might be walking on the water and not know it and then suddenly know it and drown."

Flannery O'Connor's description of the boyhood struggles of Hazel Motes in *Wise Blood* (New York: Farrar, Straus & Giroux, 1962, p. 22) is a reminder of our struggles with race. We have refused to believe that God has power over the quagmire of race; like Motes, we have tried to make it on our own way. That path is a return to the power of race that has plagued us from the European beginnings of this country. As O'Connor reminds us, though, God has not yet given up on us and beckons us to come to the waters. Even as the power of race grips us more tightly, strengths and possibilities are available to us. There is still a strong and increasing black consciousness that is a long way from being crushed and refuses to be defined by a white agenda. There are white people who want to affirm equality, who want to do the right thing, and who seek to reject the system of race.

The first step in confronting race is to acknowledge the system of race. White people are extremely reluctant to admit that the system of race still exists and that we gain great benefits from it. This study has been *relentless* about the power of race in our society, not because black people must be uplifted and white people degraded but because white people want so much to deny the power of the system of race. It is as if the mule must be hit in the head to get its attention. So it is with white people and race. White denial is such that a strong and relentless campaign must be carried out merely to get white people to acknowledge that the system of race exists, much less try to change the system of race.

This is the beginning—for white people to acknowledge that a system of race exists, that it has existed for centuries, and that we gain great benefits from it. It is difficult to begin this journey; the old maxim that "the longest journey begins with one step" applies here as well. That first step is enormous—to acknowledge the existence and the power of the system of race.

I suggest that race rivals class and gender in terms of power to classify humanity in our culture. Because all three of these categories are important, it is worthwhile to look briefly at their intersection to realize how powerful the category of race really is. As a comfortable white male, I approach this intersection with great trepidation, for I have some awareness of the power of my personal categories to shape my thinking and reflections. I feel like Hazel Motes, trying to get rid of that ragged figure who calls me to the waters, but come I must to the waters.

The relationship between race and class has been complex throughout the European history of this nation. Part of the American dream was the affirmation of the vision of equality. The Europeans who came to this country became Americans by seeking to leave class behind and affirming the idea of the equal dignity of each person. A European could come to this country without being totally constrained by class status. There was opportunity here, and with hard work and a bit of luck, one could break the chains of class. The vision of America was a country without a peasant class. The idea of equality was at the center of the dream of America, and it still is.

The *reality* of America has been otherwise. While we did not have an official peasant class, we did have a mechanism for providing cheap labor: slavery. The institution of slavery provided the cheap labor, but it also clashed with the ideal of equality. If one of our core ideals was the equal dignity of all people, how could we have slaves? Wasn't this a return to the class consciousness of that European past we wanted to leave behind? The problem was solved by strengthening the idea of racial classification. The idea of race had already been developed to justify European colonization of the world. We took it further in this country to be able to have both the cheap labor provided by slavery and the power of the idea of equality. The institution of slavery did not clash with the idea of equality because those held as slaves were not considered to be human beings on the same order as Europeans or white people.

This development of the idea of race in America was also useful in disguising class barriers among white people. The system of race is used as part of the method in which whites who are poor are kept in poverty. Those whites whose labor and land are exploited and who are kept in poverty are consoled by the idea of race. They may be poor, but at least they are not black. The white person who is poor tends to believe that he or she has more in common with the white president of a large corporation or university than with the black person closer to him or her in class status.

Some have argued that the system of racial classification is really rooted in class warfare. It is true that race and economic class are inextricably bound in our culture. American slavery and the legal segregation that followed were based on racial classification. Although slavery was an economic system designed to bring benefits to certain classes of people, the limitations on who benefited from slave labor were not determined by class status. They were determined by racial status. To argue, then, that race is only an extension of the class system is to miss a large point: Race has a life of its own, capable of destroying movements that challenge class status in this country.

From Tom Watson to Orval Faubus (whose father was a socialist) to George Wallace, the populist cause of uniting the poor in opposition to the affluent has been overwhelmed by race. When it comes down to getting the votes, the white populist has almost always played the race card. This same race affliction plagues Jesse Jackson and the Rainbow Coalition. The coalition has never caught fire in this country because the white part of the coalition remains uncomfortable with a black man leading it. I am not contending that a black man should not lead the coalition. I am saying that until white discomfort with this situation is put on the table, there will be no significant union of blacks and whites to fight class oppression.

There cannot be real progress in relation to the power of class until the power of race is acknowledged and confronted. In this sense, race is primary. It is fundamental to the powerlessness of the poor, both black and white. The refusal to acknowledge the primacy of race has doomed every poor peoples' movement in this country, from the Populists of the last century to the labor and socialist movements of this century. Race has a life of its own.

Gender is also a fundamental category by which one's humanity is classified in this society. For women, oppression by gender is a daily experience in this country and worldwide. Indeed, one could argue that oppression by gender is the primary oppression on a worldwide scale. In this society, however, race rivals gender oppression and is used to undergird it. This was brought home to me in a recent conversation with a white woman friend. She agreed with me that race was powerful, but she also felt that I had underestimated the power of gender. Since I am a white man, it would be foolish not to give her idea serious consideration. In discussing this, she indicated that women live in daily exposure to oppression as women because classification by gender is so central. She cited a recent move that her family had made from a racially mixed neighborhood to a virtually all-white neighborhood. Their family had made the move because of her growing sense of vulnerability to men. I asked her if there were men in her new neighborhood, and she said that there were. I said, "But, they aren't black men, are they?" She said, "No, they aren't." I replied, "So, it's not a question of just men but rather *black* men that has increased your sense of the power of gender." She said, "Yes, it is the black men...I had not thought about how powerful race is. Indeed, statistically, I am much more likely to be harmed by a white man, but it is black men that I fear the most."

Angela Davis makes a similar point in her book *Women, Race, & Class* (New York: Random House, 1983, pp. 177-183). She notes that feminist writers such as Susan Brownmiller, Shulamith Firestone, and Diana Russell obscure the real social causes of rape and other forms of male oppression by emphasizing the alleged tendency of black men to want to rape white women. This emphasis fails to understand how important the role of the image of the black rapist has been in the system of race. This image has been central in the oppression of black men by white society. In emphasizing the black rapist, Davis points out, these feminists severely weaken the case for solidarity among *all* women in response to male oppression of women. Darker women are forced to choose between race and gender because of the lack of awareness among white women of the power that race continues to exert in their push for freedom from male oppression. White women often wonder why black women seem to be less sensitive to gender issues. The truth is that black women tend to pull back from gender issues when their white sisters exhibit a recalcitrance on race. It becomes a vicious cycle—black women see white women as still clinging to racism, and white women see black women as soft on male oppression.

Patriarchy and race are intertwined in this culture, and women of darker color and women called white will never be able to forge a movement powerful enough to confront patriarchy until the power of race is first acknowledged and confronted. Just as race is used to disguise class barriers among white people, so also is race used to disguise the power of gender among women. Race is used to separate women from one another; until its power is acknowledged by women, few lasting steps can be taken to improve conditions for women.

The intersection of race, class, and gender has much to teach us. For example, the abuse of women was perceived early on as a class problem. It was claimed that only lower-class men abused women. If we could just raise the educational level and the class status of these poor men, their loutish behavior would stop. Over several decades, the testimony of many courageous women has forced us to see the difficult truth: Abuse of women happens regardless of class, education, or professional status. Abuse of women is epidemic, and the argument that gender oppression is related only to class misses the mark entirely. To reduce male domination of women to class analysis is to miss a large point—it happens in almost every society in the world. This insight is useful in a similar analysis of class and race, but it is often overlooked because of the unresolved issues over race in the feminist movement. In the intersection of race, gender, and class, class often is pushed to the side, unspoken but divisive in its power. It cannot be overemphasized: Until the power of racial classification is acknowledged and confronted, the power of economic class and patriarchy cannot be successfully challenged. We must come to the waters. In this country, racial classification is primary. Whether it is more important than class or gender is not as important as the acknowledgment that race remains primary in our society. Despite the Civil War, despite the civil rights movement, race remains primary, its power unabated. We must come to these waters, as bitter as they are, for they offer us the possibility of healing.

CHAPTER 8

"My Name Is Legion"

Race is primary in our society, and race is a social and political construct. The system of racial classification in this country was established centuries ago by Europeans to justify exploitation of other lands and people. Race is not a scientific or biological category. Racial classification is not rooted in scientific analysis of the branches of the human family. Racial classification is rooted in access to social, economic, and political power, and it has changed dramatically over the years. When I was in high school, the "scientific" categories of races were only three main branches: Caucasoid, Negroid, and Mongoloid. Now, there are many more branches such as Hispanic, Asian, Native American, and African-American. I have even seen Jewish in a list of racial classifications!

Racial classification has been and will ever be fluid. It will be this way not because of the continuing development of more precise measuring tools in the sciences but because racial classification describes who should have access to power and opportunity. The meaning of race as access to power was revealed once again to me last fall when I filled out a form for a major university at which I was to teach as adjunct faculty. Five races were listed under the "Race Code" section: White non-Hispanic, Black non-Hispanic, Hispanic, Asian/Pacific, and American Indian/Alaskan Native. Several things jumped out at me. Why did the categories of Asian and Indian have place names while

White and Black had no place names? Why was "Other" not a possibility?

Most of all, I noticed the "non-Hispanic," which followed "White" and "Black." Why was this attached? The dictionary defines Hispanic as the Latin name for the Iberian Peninsula (Spain and Portugal). As a noun, it means "a usually Spanish-speaking person of Latin American origin who lives in the U.S." Now its meaning becomes clearer. Because of the significant amount of intermarriage, it is no longer certain who is white and who is black from countries south of the United States. Dark-skinned folk of Hispanic origin might be mistaken for those of African descent. The Hispanic label also gives us a clue—somewhere, sometime, Hispanics had some white or European ancestry, so they are different from black people. Despite this strange journey to distinguish white from black for those born south of the U.S. border, people classified as Hispanic often suffer as much discrimination in this country as those classified as black.

That brings up one more point in relation to the "scientific" basis of racial classification. I was part of a records committee at our denomination's national assembly in Wichita in June 1994. People of Hispanic origin brought up the issue of their desire to have a more finely drawn racial category than Hispanic on our reporting forms. They wanted the one category of Hispanic to be broken down into two categories: Hispanic-white and Hispanic-black. Why? They had correctly perceived that one's consciousness and access to power is decidedly different if one is classified as white instead of black.

This is a tortuous example of the fluidity of racial classification, but I hope that its very difficulty exposes the roots of race. Race is not an objective category of classification for human beings. It is a subjective category that seeks to limit access to power and opportunity and thus tends to define who in the human family is worth more and who is worth less.

There are no white people, no black people, no yellow people. There are certainly many different cultures, many different facial and hair features, many darker and lighter skin colors. None of them has anything to do with race. White and black have to do with power and access, not biological or even cultural differences. In this sense, to be classified as white or black is extremely important; but the classification system itself is also extremely arbitrary. That is why miscegenation laws were so strong until only twenty-eight years ago. If there was too much intermarriage, the categories of white and black would disappear. One could no longer tell who was white and who was black.

Although race is primal, its validity as a system of classification is arbitrary and prejudicial. Even though we may accept the idea of the arbitrary nature of race, many of us who would challenge its power have accepted it as a system of classification. We speak of "racial justice," improving "race relations," or overcoming "racial discrimination." We fail to notice that merely putting the discussion in these terms is losing half the battle for justice. Reform of the system of racial classification is not possible because the very purpose of this system is to determine who has access to power. As long as race remains central, there will be gates to power that open for some and close for others. Our goal is not to reform the system of race so that darker people are seen as equals. Our goal is to abolish the system of race so that darker people are seen as *people*. The system of race is an arbitrary creation for the purposes of oppression and exploitation. In this sense, it is not helpful in the long run to believe that we have solved the problems of racism by changing the name from "nigger" to "Negro," "black," or even "African-American." This is only a small, first step, and it must be seen as the beginning of a journey toward abolishing the system of race rather than reforming it.

Because race remains so central and volatile, I am offering two disclaimers relative to the idea of abolishing race. First, some may hear this as an unrealistic call to deny differences among human beings. It is not that at all. There are clearly different hair textures, skin colors, weights, heights, and so forth, and these differences should be celebrated as part of the great variety of life that God has given us. The purpose of racial classification, however, is not to note the difference in human beings. Its purpose is to determine who is a higher order of humanity and who is a lesser order.

Second, race has great resiliency, and because of that, we must not seek to abolish it without first acknowledging that it exists. We must be realistic about how deep its roots are in our lives. It will take long, hard work to abolish race in this nation, and until we do, we must seek to be ever mindful of its continuing power and presence. We all are aware of people in this society who say, "I do not see race—I see people." That is simply not true. We all see race first—that is its purpose, and that is its power. It takes only a few probing questions to determine the power of race in our lives—questions such as Where do you live? Where do you go to church or synagogue or mosque? Where do your children go to school? These kinds of questions reveal that we continue to use racial categories to order our lives. When we speak of the abolition of race, we must be careful to see that as a goal rather than as a pronouncement. If we only pronounce race as abolished without wrestling with its power in an open process, we will simply drive it underground and make it even more powerful. We must name it and acknowledge it before we can seek to abolish it.

What would our society look like if the system of race were named and then abolished? To acknowledge the system of race and seek its abolition, we will need to reorient our way of thinking. Rather than seeing life and its different cultures as competitive, we can begin to see them as complementary. The family of humanity is a tapestry, not a battlefield or a race. There will always be competition, just as there will always be sibling rivalry. Unless a common thread can be found, however, that competition and rivalry will tear the family asunder. The world crises that we now face demand a sense of cooperation, not competition.

A second benefit that will come from naming and then banishing race is that all people would be welcomed into the family of humanity. People of darker color have been denied entrance into this family because they have been seen as less than human. To abolish the idea of race is to welcome all peoples into the tapestry of humanity. Not only darker people would be welcomed back into humanity—white people would return also. In the system of race, we white people have set ourselves aside as normative and in this way have cut ourselves off from the family of humanity. We see this in many ways, but nowhere is it clearer than in the language of the system of race. There are white people and there are people of color. White people want to affirm that we have no color and thus are not like the rest of humanity. People of color, then, are somehow less than this norm. Yet, whites have color! White people belong to the family of humanity, but we are not the norm for that family. Although I have used black and white as descriptive terms in this study, I do not use white and people of color. There is no such distinction. White people must not set up "people of color, ethnics, racial ethnics," or "minorities" (especially "minority," for it is a term that applies to those who cannot take care of themselves). "Lighter skin" and "darker skin" are more accurate descriptions, but they do not touch the issues of power and access. To name the system of race and then to work for its abolition, therefore, is to offer white people, also, an invitation to join the human family.

Being welcomed into the human family is a strange proposition for white people. We have believed for so long that we are the norm, and it is threatening to hear that we are only *part* of the tapestry of life rather than the *center* of it. The first steps in rejoining the human family will be scary—we whites do not know if we have a culture or a set of beliefs. In this sense, white people have been invented, just as black people have been invented. White people moan constantly about the dangers of pluralism and multiculturalism. We are told that our values will be lost or relativized when many cultures try to come together. Underlying this lament is the belief that white, European values are the norm for all of humanity and the belief that we cannot possibly learn anything about values from other cultures. On one hand, this is laughable. We who are white stole this country and murdered the native people who were here, stole other people from Africa to provide cheap labor, and continue to lead the world in the irresponsible use of precious natural resources. We have plenty to learn from other cultures!

Why do we lament this opportunity to learn from other cultures? On a more powerful and less conscious level, we have been taught by the system of race that we are the best, the highest order of humanity. We believe that no one from another race can teach us anything about values because we are the value of humanity. We are the norm of humanity against which all others are to be measured. Our ability to respond to a call for naming race and then seeking to abolish it is limited by our sense that others need change, not us.

To help us who name ourselves white hear and accept the call to name racism, I offer two models that can assist in this perilous journey. One is therapeutic or medical—the idea that racism is a disease and must be treated as such. The other is theological or religious—the idea that racism is demonic and must be exorcised as such. We will look at both models, for each has its virtues and vices.

The therapeutic model comes directly from our time—we are in an age that sees the problems of life as diseases that can be treated. Until very recently, this model claimed that the patient (or host of the disease) had very little to contribute to the healing process. The patient, or the one afflicted, was seen as a passive host. The struggle for health would be waged between the doctor (priest or shaman) and the weapons of drugs versus the impersonal germ or organism attacking us. The word "patient," therefore, has come to describe the one hosting the disease. A patient is one who waits for the result, with an emphasis on passivity, while the doctor wages the struggle on our behalf. In this sense, the will, identity, or self-knowledge of the patient are relatively unimportant or even detrimental.

This idea of patient passivity is being reconsidered today. Evidence is mounting that will and self-knowledge are important in the healing process. The attacking organism is still seen as impersonal (and thus not "evil"), but the patient is now seen as an active participant in the healing process rather than as a passive battleground. Whether it is cancer, heart disease, diabetes, glaucoma, colitis, or a myriad of other diseases, the will of the patient has taken on much more importance. It is in this light that we will consider racism as a disease of white people.

I emphasize "a disease of white people" because, by definition, people of darker color cannot have racism. They can be and are prejudiced, but they are not racists because they have no power in the system of race. There is certainly discrimination by skin color in the black community, but it is not racism—it is prejudice. White people are loathe to hear this distinction be-cause we want to believe that the system of race has equality in it, that black people as well as white people can be racist.

This may seem to be a minor point. Does it matter whether we say that black people are racists or that they are prejudiced? And, if we say that black people can't be racist, aren't we denying the obvious truth that black people often see white people only as being white and deny humanity to whites as well? It is true that black people have learned to look at white people by racial classification first and humanity second. We who are white have taught them well. There are two major differences, however.

First, black people have learned to judge by skin color be-cause it is a matter of survival. They have learned that trusting white people is dangerous, just as touching fire is dangerous. Most of the African-American people I know long to have the system of race abolished so they will be seen as human beings first. Yet, as long as the system of race exists, they have learned that they must be very careful when encountering those seen as white. This is not racism—it is survival. This survival syndrome can and does lend itself to extreme positions in which whites are seen as devils and monsters. This is a reaction to racism, how-ever, not a manifestation of racism. Malcolm X went through this process in his journey of education about the system of racial classification. As he discovered what had been done to his own sense of humanity and that of his brothers and sisters, he lashed out in anger and frustration and a sense of injustice. He came to recognize that it was not helpful to call anybody a devil, but he did not deny or rebuke the anger. It is a necessary part of the journey to health.

We who are white still may ask, Whatever you say about Malcolm X, black people are still judging by skin color, by racial classification, just as white people, aren't they? Aren't they doing the same thing to white people that white people are doing to them? What is the difference? Here, the second differ-ence between white and black participation in the system of race must be lifted up. White people cite "black racism" as a reason for avoiding white responsibility for the creation of the system of race. If everyone is equally racist, white responsibility for this system can be avoided. Racism then turns out to be a universal, human problem in which everyone participates. White participation in racism, then, is just one group among many. To follow this line of thinking is to escape white responsibility for creating and maintaining the system of race. Racism is not a universal trait shared by all humanity. It is a creation of a particular people designed for particular purposes in a particular historical context. It is the responsibility of those who have taken the name white.

To make this claim about the particularity of racism is not to deny the universality of categories used by certain groups around the world to strip the humanity of other groups. That universal practice, however, is not what is meant by racism. Racism is a creation of white people, and white people must be held solely responsible for its continuing power. This is not to say that black people and other people of darker color do not have major roles to play in the abolition of racism and the system of race—they do—it is to say that the major responsibility for the continuing power of racism and the abolition of this system belongs to white people. With this understanding, let us now return to the idea of racism as a disease of white people.

Within the model of racism as disease, there are many possibilities. I want to suggest two: cancer and addiction. As many have pointed out, the resurgence of the system of race in our history is not like a heart attack that strikes suddenly and changes everything immediately. The resurgence of the system of race is more like a cancer that grows slowly and spreads over much of the body before it presents its symptoms clearly. August Meier points out that the system of race did not reestablish itself overnight following Reconstruction. It was gradually put back together, piece by piece (p. 20). We are seeing that same gradual development in our time in the white response to the civil rights movement, but there is still time to intervene before this cancer is fatal to human relations, before it can consume the entire body. Early detection is important in the treatment of cancer. So it is with the system of race. The longer a person ignores the warning signs of cancer, the more tenacious the disease becomes and the more resistant to treatment and eradication.

The racism/cancer analogy is also helpful to individuals in

another way. The most difficult part of individual white people's acknowledging the system of race and our culpability in it is being overwhelmed by guilt and shame. We believe that we are bad people. The racism/cancer analogy tends to take away the guilt that so often paralyzes us. Racism doesn't just leap on a white person at some stage in life. It gradually develops; it is learned at an early age, often before the child even has the ability to know it, much less question it. Although there is evidence that some cancers are related to the life-style habits of individuals, cancer is still seen as a disease that strikes individuals regardless of their habits or their worth. So it is with racism—whether the white person is a good person or not is immaterial. Racism strikes all white people—with no exceptions. There is no white person untouched by the power of the system of race. To be healed from cancer often means changing our habits, even though we may not share total blame individually for the development of those habits. As with someone who has cancer, it is crucial to take immediate responsibility for the current manifestations of the disease of racism in our lives, whether we can be blamed for the development of those manifestations or not.

Understanding racism as a form of cancer can assist white people in acknowledging it and seeking to eradicate it. Early detection, willingness to admit its presence, and willingness to change the way one lives to find healing—all are helpful in confronting the system of race and seeking to abolish it. The system of race spreads like a cancer, it eats us up as a society, and it is just as deadly. The racism/cancer analogy has one important shortcoming, however; it does not adequately address the individual will and issues of personal identity needed to eradicate the system of race. For that missing ingredient, we must turn to the second therapeutic model of racism as disease: addiction.

If studying the white response to the civil rights movement demonstrates anything at all, it should be that white people are addicted to the system of race and have the classic symptoms of addiction. The individual seems unable to control the manifestations of the disease, the disease is related to social factors, and the maintenance of the disease results from a complex interaction between the individual will and an invading agent or substance ("Racism as a Disease," *Journal of Counseling and Development,* Sept. /Oct. 1991, p. 210).

Addiction as a therapeutic model for racism is helpful because it acknowledges that an individual is invaded by a foreign agent (system of race) and that the strength of the foreign agent is related to the will of the individual. As with addiction, racism enters the individual in a slightly benign way. The substance provides some relief, and the individual begins a journey of dependence on the substance. That journey leads to a series of destructive consequences for the individual and those around her or him. If individuals are to move back toward health, they must first confront their dependence on the substance. Until this first step is taken, very little treatment will be effective. The individual must be willing to make a first step of acknowledgment: I am an addict, and I want to change. This involves an act of the will because the patient is no longer seen as a passive host for a foreign agent. The patient becomes an active participant in eradicating the disease.

This model is helpful in approaching the system of race. The first step for white people is to acknowledge an addiction to race—addiction as individuals, addiction as a group. White people are hooked on race, and until that dependence—that addiction—is acknowledged, all efforts at reform or change will fail. Addiction as a model is helpful because it agrees that the host of the disease did not start out with evil intent or even culpability. As children, white people learn to participate in the system of race long before they are able to stand up and resist it. The model of addiction, however, does not leave out the will, as other disease models tend to do. Addiction asserts that if individuals are to move toward health, they must first acknowledge their own responsibility for the current existence of the disease, regardless of who or what is responsible for the development of the disease in them.

Though the society or their family may share culpability in the development of the addiction, the continued use of the addictive substance or agent is now the responsibility of the addict. The beginning step to health is to resist shifting blame to others. This is especially helpful in the system of race, for white people avoid acknowledging addiction to race by blaming people of darker color for its effects. Just as an addict blames others for her or his disease, so white people blame people of darker color for the system of race. It is the addict's classic flight from responsibility. Very little progress can be made until the addict accepts responsibility for her or his conduct.

The model of racism as addiction is helpful because it acknowledges that even though individuals are invaded by an agent beyond their knowledge or initial ability to control, the continued use of that substance is under their will and control. White people learn racism at an early age, but white people are not hopelessly addicted to race. Though its power is strong and pervasive, racism can be controlled and even eradicated. It is extremely difficult to do this on an individual level, however. To deal with this social dimension of the system of race, we must depart from the therapeutic model and move into the mysterious land of the spirit and religion: racism as demonic possession.

To talk about demonic possession is to open up many difficult areas. In brief, this model emphasizes that there is a power that can overtake individuals, a power that grows as groups of people appropriate it. In group or social psychology, it is that dimension that never supersedes the autonomy of the individual but exerts strong influence on the individual. To call it demonic possession is not to imply that there is a demon with a personality lurking out in the air waiting to conquer individuals. It is to assert that there is a power that can possess individuals and groups and cause them to do terrible things. How else can one explain a good and decent white father who nonetheless participates in a lynching? How else can one explain a white banker, a good mother to her children, who nonetheless refuses to approve a loan to a black family because she decides it is a bad risk, despite the family member(s)' having an acceptable job and income? It would be easier to dismiss them as evil people, but that diagnosis misses the reality and offers little hope for change.

To use demonic possession as a model for dealing with racism is to acknowledge that history and ambition build up a structure of the perception of reality that impinges on white individuals. The demon has no existence outside this structure; but once the structure begins to take shape, it develops an existence that is at once independent of and yet dependent on that structure.* The demon seems to have independent existence because it both gains and generates power from the structure of racism. At the same time, demonic power always remains dependent on the structure for its existence. If the structure is dismantled, the demonic power will cease to exist.

The importance of this model in helping whites to deal with the system of race is in its insight into the intersection of individual and community. A child born into a family in the United States has no idea that there are such racial categories as black and white. They are learned categories imposed on the world that greets the child. They are imposed not because each individual white family is evil but because each individual white family is possessed by the demon of race. It is not a possession that causes whites to foam at the mouth or to turn their heads 360 degrees; it is a possession that causes whites to learn that people of darker color, especially black people, are not human beings as white people are. It is also a possession that causes white people to assert that we are not part of the common thread of humanity. Rather, we are special; indeed, we are at the top because we have won the race. Once again, this model explains why it is so important to be able to determine who is white, so that whites will know who to accept and who to reject.

The model of demonic possession is helpful because, like the cancer and addiction models, it allows the individual to retain a sense of integrity or goodness while also acknowledging that one needs treatment. The added dimension of the model of demonic possession is that it emphasizes the existence of a power that can overcome an individual and make her or him join with other individuals to do terrible things. This model acknowledges that the system of race cannot be abolished by each individual white person deciding to give it up. Its strength is too deep and great, and it must be viewed in a systemic

---

* For insight on demons, see Walter Wink, "Unmasking the Powers" (Philadelphia: Fortress Press, 1986), especially ch. 2.

fashion—a demon has been created that will take both individual and community efforts to eradicate.

For those puzzled by this model, I want to offer an example. Anyone who wants to confront the power of the system of race would do well to read the story called the "Gerasene demoniac" in the Bible. It is found in the books of Mark and Luke. I will concentrate on the Marcan version (5:1-20). This story provides great insight into the system of race, whether one is Christian, generally religious, or other. I am again greatly indebted to Walter Wink's insights into this story. In this story, Jesus travels across a lake for the first time into Gentile territory. There he encounters a wild man in Gerasa, a man who is naked and lives among the dead, a man who bruises himself with stones and howls on the mountain. He prefers the dead to the living, but he has incredible life force. His passion and power are so great that no chains can hold him. The community is greatly threatened by this "demoniac" and has sought to chain him up, but nothing can hold him.

When Jesus arrives, the man runs to worship him but also begs Jesus not to torment him like everyone else does. Jesus seeks to heal the man, but the healing is difficult. To be healed, the man must give his name. The name he gives is not a human name, but "Legion." "Legion" not only denotes many—it also names the most disciplined and powerful military unit the Western world has ever known: the Roman legion. To be healed of his demonic possession, the man first must name the demon. The name he gives speaks of the depth and the power of the demon—we are many, and we will crush you. The name he gives is the name of the systemic oppressor: Legion. He must acknowledge that he has given up much of his own identity and has taken on the identity of the demon—the Roman legion that oppresses his people.

This story offers great insights into the encounter of black and white people with the system of race. The demonic influence of racism often forces black people and other people of darker color into the self-destructive behavior seen in this man from Gerasa. The demonic power of racism often causes white people to give up their identity and take on the identity of the demon, as this man in Gerasa has done. This story also acknowledges the life force of those who are oppressed. The man from Gerasa will not be completely captured by the demonic power—no chains can hold him. The story points us to the continuing struggle between race and equality and to the life force of the people that whites would seek to destroy. This story exposes demonic possession as that which takes over part of our identity and leads us into behavior that is destructive to others and ourselves. So it is with the system of race. It must be named, and our dependence on it must be acknowledged. Only when this first step is taken can the healing process begin, as the story demonstrates.

The insight of this biblical story does not stop with the necessity of naming the demonic possession to begin healing. It also acknowledges the cost of healing. As with all demons, they cannot exist without a structure to support them. When the demons see that Jesus intends to heal this man, they beg Jesus to let them inhabit something else, lest they cease to exist. In a bizarre twist, Jesus accepts their request and allows them to leave the man and enter a herd of pigs. The pigs go crazy and rush off the hillside into the water and drown, taking the demons with them.

What is going on here? Why in the world is this included in this story? It seems so cruel to the innocent pigs, and it seems so incredibly destructive. Like a Flannery O'Connor tale, however, this story is not without humor. Why would Jesus allow the pigs to be possessed? Perhaps one reason is that he is Jewish and pigs are unclean to him. From this viewpoint, the loss of the pigs is not a great loss.

There are three insights for us in this second part of the story. First, although demons take on power of their own, they cannot exist apart from the structures that gave rise to them. The demonic power of the Roman legion cannot exist without the structures that support it, without individuals and communities who continue to say yes to it. Second, demonic possession always leads to destructive power and death. The man bruises himself and howls in agony—the pigs rush to their death. Third, the cleansing of demonic possession is a struggle. It is costly—in this case, the cost is a herd of pigs. There is no magic, easy formula for healing from the demonic possession. It is a struggle.

The second part of the story again offers us great insights into the struggle with the system of race. The demonic power of race is primal, but it cannot exist unless white people say yes to it. Race has come into being because a certain group of people wanted to exploit other people, and this category was invented to justify that exploitation. It continues to operate at this very moment because white individuals and white communities say yes to it, further deepening its power and hold on our society. Yet, for all its depth and power, it can be exorcised because it has no independent existence of its own. Second, the system of race leads to destructive behavior for all. Whites benefit greatly from the system of race, and blacks are pushed to bruise themselves by the system. Whites, too, are bruised, because we give over our human identity to the system of race. Rather than being part of the tapestry of humanity with our particular heritage and culture, we give up that identity to become white. For all people in this society, the system of race leads to destruction and death. A third insight of this part of the story is that healing is costly. It means realigning priorities and relearning how to perceive the world. The system of race has provided and continues to provide great benefits to those who have allowed themselves to be identified as white. To change this demonic possession, those benefits must change. It will be a costly change, as we see in this story.

The third part of this story reminds us of the dynamics of the community in demonic possession. After the man is healed and the pigs are driven to death, the herdsmen run into town to tell everybody what has happened. They find the man who used to be crazy and naked now healed and clothed, and they see the cost of the healing—a herd of pigs. Rather than rejoicing in finding a way to cure demonic possession, the community is stunned and frightened. Rather than urging Jesus to stay and heal others, they demand that he leave their community. The healing is too costly—2,000 pigs for one man? Jesus does leave, and opportunities for further healing seem to pass.

The last part of the story reminds us that the power of the system of race is derived not only from a group of individuals who come to see themselves as white. It is also derived from the community, structures, and history that come to be identified as white. To seek healing from the power of race means that an individual identified as white must not only confront one's own personal history and presence but also the entire history and presence of the community that has developed around the identification of being white. It is no easy task because it requires that individuals and communities confront their own histories. Whereas individuals can sometimes gather the courage to encounter themselves, the healing in this process is often stopped when the community is threatened by the individual and seeks to ostracize or crush the individual. For example, many of us who are white and who have tried to combat racism have experienced the pain of estrangement, and sometimes rejection, by our families and white friends. We are sometimes seen as traitors to the race.

The man from Gerasa had perhaps attempted to get his friends and his community to confront the demonic power of the Roman legion. The result was not a genuine encounter and healing—the result was the ostracism and further demonic possession of the man who would speak for healing. In this way, the initial fears of the community about healing are correct—it would be costly. As so often happens in demonic possession, the community is successful in isolating the individual and making the individual seem to be the crazy one, instead of acknowledging the craziness of the demonic possession of the community. When Jesus exposes this process, the community urges him to leave. They prefer crazy individuals they can ostracize.

The final part of this story reminds us of this interplay between the individual and the community. Having been ostracized once by the community because he raised the name of the demon, the man from Gerasa begs Jesus to allow him to leave the community and go with Jesus. He has already felt the wrath of the community and has been driven crazy once; he does not want to go through that again. Jesus refuses his request, however. Jesus may seem cold and indifferent here. Doesn't he know that the man may be crushed again? Jesus is not being cruel; he is being hopeful. If the demonic possession is to come to an end, it will come from this man's returning to his community as a witness to the power of healing. Jesus sends the man back to say that although the power of demonic possession is great, it is not ultimate or final. Though healing is costly, it is possible; and in the long run, it is less costly. The man goes back to his community, and witnesses to the power of his healing.

This final insight is important as we struggle with the system of race. The community of people who have identified themselves as white have a great investment in not having the system of race named and exposed as demonic possession. When an individual, especially a white individual, does so, she or he is immediately isolated as a troublemaker or crazy person. Such individuals are ostracized and dismissed as disloyal to their people or are seen as threats to themselves and to the community. This story speaks to us of the necessity for these individuals to persevere, to seek out others, and to continue naming the demon, as did this man from Gerasa. It is the only road to health.

These models of cancer, addiction, and demonic possession are various attempts to help white people come to terms with the power of the system of race. The system must be named and acknowledged, and it must be abolished. We individuals who claim whiteness as part of our identity need not flagellate ourselves for discovering that we are part of the system of race and continue to perpetuate it. The models of disease and possession should encourage white people to encounter and acknowledge our participation in the system of race. To discover this participation does not mean that the individual is bad or evil but that he or she has come under the power of a foreign agent or a demon. It is vital that we accept responsibility for our continuing participation in the system and for beginning the healing process. Only in naming and accepting responsibility for our own participation can white people begin to dismantle the system of race.

CHAPTER 9

"We All…Everyone of Us"

We all, everyone of us,
*Have to come home again.**

This song by Sweet Honey in the Rock reminds me of the longing, meaning, and destination of our journey: home. The most influential theologian in the history of the Christian church, an African named Augustine, put it a different way: "Almighty God, you have made us for yourself, and our hearts are restless till they find their rest in you."

All of us want to go home. We want to find our way back to that fork where we lost our way. Though there are many reasons for feeling lost in this culture, such as individualism and materialism, the system of race is a central one. It is the first one that must be encountered if we are to find our way home. Our history has taught us that we are loathe to encounter the system of race, but our history has also made clear that the struggle over it will not go away. Our most recent history tells us that we are in a dangerous time, a time similar to that following Reconstruction, when we allowed the system of race to regain its power. If race

---

* Bernice Johnson Reagon, from the album "We all…Everyone of Us" by Sweet Honey in the Rock (Chicago: Songtalk Publishing Co. and Flying Fish Records, 1983).

regains its power—and it is seeking to do so at this very moment—then we will be a long way from home.

In the previous chapter, we looked at some general ways to begin going back to the fork we reached at the end of the civil rights movement. Now, we will look at some specific ways for people who have identified themselves as white to begin to dismantle the system of race. It is white people who created and now maintain this system, and it is "white" people who are called to dismantle it. This is not to say that people of darker color are not important in the encounter with race—they are important. However, the system of race is not the responsibility of black people; it is a creation by people of lighter color who have taken on the demonic name of white.

The first step sounds simple, but it is profound and complex: White people must begin to see people of darker color, especially black people, as human beings. This seems simple, but we must remember that the entire system of race in this country is built on denying the humanity of African-Americans. This is fundamental, as elementary as learning how to crawl.

No person who considers himself or herself white is exempt from this elemental process. Many white people stake a claim that they are not influenced by the system of race, that they are not racist. This is a lie at worst and self-deception at best. No one in this society is immune from this demonic possession of race, whether part of the KKK or a member of the most progressive group in society. All who claim the name white must realize that there are no exemptions. To be identified as white is to deny the humanity of others—it is as tautological as $1 + 1 = 2$. If you are reading this book and consider yourself white, you must start at this elementary but profoundly disturbing step.

This means that when white people encounter black people, the first impulse must not be fear, awe, or anxiety. The first impulse must be a sense of community: There goes a person just like me, with the same family struggles, finitude, hopes, disappointments, and joys. Whites have been trained to see people of darker color with a sense of distance: They are not like me. To overcome this will take some specific, elementary work. To encounter a black person is to encounter a person, a human being first and foremost. It will take relearning for white people—like learning to walk all over again. It is a process of trial and error, a couple of steps, then a fall, but a determination to get up again and keep trying.

The importance and the necessity of this first step cannot be overestimated. It is a simple process, but it is profound. Its simplicity should not hide its difficulty. Almost every part of our society proclaims that white people are of a different caliber of humanity—on a higher plane—than others. The only way to unlearn this basic lie is to go through a simple process of naming it, recognizing it, and changing the behavior. It can be unlearned, but we who identify ourselves as white must start with the stuff of recognition. We have created and continue to maintain a system of race that denies the humanity of darker people. This is not a general, theoretical approach. It is a daily, concrete reality of life as a white person.

Perhaps the best approach for white people to unlearn racism is to say "I am a recovering racist." There is no magic formula for doing this. It begins in recognition and in naming. Then come the baby steps, the daily reminders to oneself to see people of darker color as human beings, people who are not first of all black or brown, but who are first of all *people*. It is a simple and fundamental step. But as is the case with any addiction, the first step to recovery is the most difficult.

Once this step has been taken, there will be many temptations to go back to the addiction. The system of race is so powerful and so pervasive in our society that no white person who wants to recover from it can ever expect to do it easily. The story of the man from Gerasa reminds us of the cost and struggle of recovery, whether from demonic possession or from addiction. There will be backsliding. White people will return to the system of race at the same time that they seek to recover from it. The point here is to be realistic. The power of race cannot be overcome easily. It will involve revelations from within and outside ourselves—revelations that make clear that race still holds great power over us. The most helpful approach is to recognize that the process will be one of fits and starts. When we white people fall back, we must not give up in despair or resignation. We must see our falls as evidence of the power of the addiction to race. It is possible to recover, but it is a continuing process, with no ending point in sight in our lifetime.

The first step, then, is to recognize the humanity of people of darker color. Once this step has been taken, the second step is to develop a fierce dedication to the idea of equality. This step applies to people of all colors and cultures. Whites must accept the driving idea of the Declaration of Independence: All people are created with equal dignity. People of darker color must not allow the system of race to crush that sense of dignity. The idea of equality has been a powerful force for change in this nation, but our history shows that it is no match for the idea of race— unless, that is, we all say yes to the self-evident truth that all people are created equal.

Wherever this fundamental idea of equality is denied in our culture, we must work to reaffirm it. It is this idea that has sometimes moved us toward the fine American vision that people are to be judged by the content of their character and not by their skin color, economic status, gender, or native origin.

We must be realistic about this second step also. Equality is a powerful idea in the American experience, but it has not been able to survive long in a struggle with the idea of race. We are living in a time of reaction to the assertion of equality's power in the civil rights movement. As we saw in Chapters 3 and 4, the signs point to a resurgence and victory for the idea of race. This victory is not yet inevitable, but for the idea of equality to retain its strength, all of us must rededicate ourselves to it. If we are able to take the first step of recognizing and naming the demon of race, we will be faithful in the struggle to maintain the power of the idea of equality. If whites do not take the first step of recognizing our own addiction to race, our efforts on behalf of equality will wilt under the heat of the power of race.

What will this dedication to equality mean in specific terms? For white people, it will mean resisting the urge to flee from people of darker color. Whether the flight is from changing neighborhoods, public schools, churches, shopping areas, mass transit, or the cities, those who see themselves as white express the power of the system of race as they flee. It is of utmost importance for whites who profess a dedication to the idea of equality that they remain in the presence of black people or other people of darker color. This is more important than picketing or participating in any other political activity for equal rights. As important and necessary as these activities are, the most important demonstration of a fierce dedication to equality among whites is to remain in the presence of black people. To accept white segregation is to return to the addiction of the system of race.

This second step of dedication to equality is like the first step—simple, yet profound and difficult. The primary response of white people to black people is flight, whether it is moving out of a neighborhood when black people move in, taking children out of public schools, locking car doors or clutching wallets more tightly in the presence of black people, or one of the many other kinds of white flight. When I drive through black neighborhoods, I still find myself checking the car doors to see if they are locked. Is this just a safety measure? You make the call: I don't do it in white neighborhoods.

I am not asking for naiveté here—the system of race has produced great anger and hostility among those classified as white and those classified as black. I am asking for a dedication to the idea of equality in all of us. I am asking us all to seek to stay with the idea of equality. If we do this, we will receive a great gift. We will begin to find the sources of our true identities. Whatever our skin colors, we all have a particular heritage and history that wait to be discovered and appropriated. It is in this discovery and integration that we find out who we are. As long as being white or black is the most important part of our identity, we will never find that real gift of being part of the human family. Because being classified as black is so crushing, those of African-American heritage are ahead of those classified as white in this area. There has been a strong development in seeking the heritage of African-Americans and other people of darker color so that what the culture sees as a negative can be seen also as powerful and positive in terms of self-definition.

Dismantling the system of race, then, would offer all of us the opportunity to expand our horizons by lifting up our particular heritage and sharing it with others. In so doing, we would all benefit. This may sound fanciful and naive, but I want to offer a concrete example. The battleground over the system of race has not been confined to the South; it has been centered in the South. It is assumed with good reason that whites and blacks are mortal enemies in the South. Yet, in important ways, those so classified may have more in common with one another as Southerners than they do with black or white people in other regions. Given its agricultural past and its slow movement into modernity, black and white Southerners share a common heritage—love of the land, a sense of the mystical and mysterious, a sense of the importance of family, and a commitment to concrete images. Were we able to dismantle the system of race, we might find more strength in one another than we can now dare imagine. This may sound hopelessly romantic, but it is true that there are many more important factors that shape human destiny than skin color. In this society, we have allowed skin color to become primary. We must make a shift so that the more important factors may come forth, factors that cut across color lines.

The first specific steps for dealing with race for those who identify themselves as white are an affirmation of the humanity of people of darker color, a strong dedication to the idea of equality, and gratitude for rediscovering our own humanity. What about people who are classified as black? Don't they have to do anything? Why are the changes in the system of race only the responsibility of white folks? There are two answers to this question. First, the system of race was created by lighter-skinned people from Europe, therefore, it is their responsibility to dismantle it. Black people can certainly agitate for its destruction, but the power for dismantling the concept of race rests on those who created it—the white people. Those classified as white cannot allow ourselves to fall back into the mainstay of the system of race, that is, to wait for black people to get ready for equality before the system of race will change. Black people have been and continue to be ready for equality. It is white people who are not ready for equality, and we must do the work necessary to get ready.

The second answer to this question is that people classified as black can continue to expose the crushing of the human spirit that is at the heart of the system of race. They can refuse to accept any white definition of themselves. They can certainly be in dialogue with others about the meaning of being human, but they risk their own sense of humanity if they allow dialogue with whites on what it means to be black. They must resist that dialogue and, fortunately for us all, many are resisting it. It cannot be overemphasized that the real question for all of us is What does it mean to be human?, not What does it mean to be black? or What does it mean to be white?

In some instances, this will mean that people of darker color will choose to segregate themselves. There is a major difference between white peoples' choosing segregation and black peoples' choosing segregation. The first group chooses it as flight from reality; the latter chooses it to find reality. For black people, segregation is sometimes the only way to recover one's humanity. We saw this in Chapter 5 in Inez Fleming's discussion related to forming a black women's group at Oakhurst Church. In a system of race that tells them they are less than human, segregation is sometimes the only way to recover that humanity. It is a risky step, of course, because white people prefer segregation; and often segregation has coincided with tremendous repression and violence from whites. Segregation by people of darker color does not mean a desire to break away from the family of humanity. Segregation by whites does mean this. Segregation by people of darker color is an attempt to recover humanity over against the lies of race.

Integration, on the other hand, does not mean that African-Americans must become white to enter the family of humanity. Rather, integration emphasizes that all of us are essential to the tapestry called humanity. If African-Americans must become white to be integrated, it does not produce the wholeness or integrity that is the root meaning of "integration"; it simply extends the power of the system of race under a new name. This is what many black leaders mean when they indicate that integration has helped to destroy institutions in the black community over the past thirty years. Integration that requires black people to accept a white definition of their identity is not integration at all; it is a failure to understand the dynamics of race.

There is a sense of "oughtness" here, to be sure. Simple justice requires that white people ought to dismantle the system of race and welcome people of darker color into the mainstream of society. If we cannot do it for ourselves and our children, what about doing it for our grandchildren and their grandchildren? This problem has plagued us for centuries, and the civil rights movement has offered us the opportunity to dismantle it. Can we do it over the next few decades and spare our great-grandchildren this same trauma and wrestling? Ought we not do it for our great-grandchildren?

While there is "oughtness" involved, there is also the possibility of a great gift. We white people who seek to eradicate the system of race will not only bestow a gift to people of darker color; we will also receive a gift ourselves, for we, too, will be welcomed into the tapestry of humanity once again. It is not just black people who are prevented from entering the human family by the system of race. White people also are prevented from doing so. The system of race dehumanizes both whites and people of darker color. Those classified as colored suffer much more than those classified as white, but everyone pays a great price—the loss of humanity—as well as suffers a tremendous sense of fear, anxiety, and hostility because of that loss. To give up race would be to gain humanity. As long as whites are so intent on keeping race, we will lift up competition and individualism as the twin pilots of our boat. The world cannot survive much longer under their direction. Cooperation must replace competition, and a genuine sense of community must overcome individualism. These are the gifts awaiting us as we dismantle the system of race.

One final step is needed to find our way home. Perhaps you have already wondered about it, but it must be addressed last because it is so powerful. Those classified as white must give up that identification and find a new language or recover an ancient one that predates the system of race.

The only purpose of the system of race has been to give choices to those classified as white and limit choices for those designated as black or colored. Those who affirm being white see it as a real category given to them by fate, God, or science. They do not see it as an evil creation, rooted in injustice and exploitation. The truth is that, although white people do not exist, the power of being classified as white is only too real and too powerful. These categories describe aspects of power; they are not scientific data. This demonic reality of the creation of white and black must be encountered by white people before it can be abolished. We dare not skip over this lightly. Those who accept the classification "white" must encounter the harmful power of the system of race. There must be authenticity in the encounter, calling not so much for shame and guilt as for acknowledgment and recognition. The power and access that derive from being classified as white must be acknowledged.

The struggle for whites to change identity will be intense, but there are great possibilities. There is the promise of authenticity as whites move through the struggle. To sense the depth of this struggle and glimpse the possibilities, I want to turn to another biblical story, this time from the Old Testament. It is the story of Jacob and Esau in chapters 25-33 of the Book of Genesis. Esau was born first, but with his brother Jacob holding his heel. Esau was the hunter and was favored by their father, Isaac. Jacob was the quieter one favored by their mother, Rebekah.

In chapter 27, we read that Isaac, who was now blind, called Esau in to ask him to prepare a favorite meal so that Isaac could give him his blessing as the elder son. Esau went out to hunt game for the meal. Rebekah had overheard the conversation, and while Esau was out hunting, she helped Jacob prepare a meal and take it in to her husband, Isaac. Jacob, disguised as Esau, went in to his father, Isaac. Isaac, unable to see, told his visitor that he smelled like Esau but sounded like Jacob. "Who are you, my son?" he asked. Jacob lied and said, "I am Esau." By this deceit, Jacob received the blessing intended for Esau. Esau soon returned and brought the meal to his father, at which time he heard the terrible news that Jacob had stolen his blessing. Isaac and Esau lamented the loss, and Esau resolved to kill his brother after the death of his father. Jacob learned of Esau's anger and fled in terror. He went to live with his mother's brother Laban. Here he sojourned for many years and learned the ways of the world through his cunning uncle.

In chapters 31 and 32, we find Jacob as a grown, mature man. Later on, he would come to be the father of the Twelve Tribes of Israel; but to do this, he first had to return home. He had been in flight for many years, and he was tired of wrestling with Laban. Moreover, he had had a dream in which God told him to go home. God told Jacob that God would make a great nation from his children. Jacob longed to go home, to find peace, to come to terms with his past and put an end to his flight. He had lied to his daddy—he had stolen from his brother. His past was weighing heavily on him, and he wanted to go home. But, before he could go home to his father's land, he first had to pass through the land of his brother Esau, the brother whom he had cheated.

Jacob hoped for the best. Genesis tells us that Jacob sent messengers ahead to his brother Esau, telling Esau that he was coming home and that he must pass through Esau's land. He also let Esau know how rich he had become. He even listed his assets—all the goats, rams, bulls, and cows. His messengers returned to Jacob with terrible news: Esau was coming to meet Jacob and was bringing 400 men with him. Jacob was scared to death. It was payback time for Jacob.

If you know the story of Jacob, you know that he was cunning. He devised a couple of plans to try to mitigate Esau's anger and destructive power. First, he would try to overwhelm Esau with gifts. Thus, he sent wave after wave after wave of people with presents for Esau, telling Esau that Jacob was close behind. This is the way that wealthy people and societies often try to end their problems and crises. If we just throw enough money at the problem, it will be solved.

Jacob prayed for deliverance, but his prayer was a flight from responsibility, not a recognition of responsibility. Jacob's prayer in chapter 32 of Genesis emphasizes God's responsibility for Jacob's predicament. Jacob muttered a few words about his unworthiness, but the tone of his prayer intended to remind God that all of this was God's responsibility. This was God's doing, the prayer insists; God must provide deliverance from Esau's power.

Nowhere in his prayer did Jacob say the truth, that he had sinned against his family. He had lied to his father and cheated his brother. He had brought destruction and disaster upon himself. He did not say, "God, I've made a terrible mess—please save me!" Instead, he blamed God for the problem and asked God to get him out of it. Jacob believed that his brother Esau was his biggest problem. If he could just find a way to get around

Esau—maybe bribe him with all these presents, maybe have a great escape by splitting up his company, maybe ask God to deliver him. If he could just get around Esau, his problem would be solved.

Jacob's problem was not Esau, however. His biggest problem was himself. Jacob was unwilling to face his own brokenness and destructiveness. In all of his scheming and praying, Jacob was unable to discern the truth. He was unable to see that what prevented him from going home was not Esau, but rather his own refusal to accept responsibility for his predicament. After all, it might have been his mother Rebekah's fault. Remember, she had helped him in the deception. She told him what to do, to put on Esau's "manly" clothing of the hunter. So, it was really his mother's fault. If she hadn't asked him to do it, he wouldn't have done it. Or, maybe it's Esau's fault. Esau had sold his birthright to Jacob—sold it cheaply, too, for a bowl of soup. Didn't that show how lightly Esau regarded everything? So Esau planted this deception in Jacob's heart. If Esau had said no to the deal, Jacob surely would have stopped. Or, maybe it was God's fault. If God hadn't asked Jacob to go home in that dream, Jacob would have remained in comfort, near Laban. As his prayer indicates, Jacob was still in flight. Even though he was headed home, he was still running away.

Yet, God was gracious to Jacob, just as God often is to us when we are broken and fleeing in anxiety and blaming God for our problem. Jacob found his answer, not in being delivered from facing Esau, but in being forced to face himself. Jacob settled down for the night. He sent everybody away from him. He needed to think about all of this—to wrestle with it. The Scriptural story in Genesis tells us that Jacob was left alone and someone came to wrestle with him in the middle of the night. It is in the nighttime that we often wrestle with our problems and with who we are. Nighttime wrestling comes just when we seek sleep; nighttime wrestling comes as we seek to find home.

So it was with Jacob. Alone and frightened, he wrestled in the middle of the night about his identity. It is not clear who came to wrestle him. It is not clear whether it was a dream or whether it actually happened outside Jacob's own psyche; but in this wrestling, Jacob found an authentic answer to his problem. The wrestling was fierce and painful. It lasted until the break of day. The easy and quick healing for which Jacob had hoped was not a possibility.

During the struggle, Jacob cried out to be blessed, "I will not let you go until you bless me." It was a calling back to the very lie itself, for this was the second time Jacob had asked to be blessed. The first time he had come to his blind father to receive the blessing of his elder brother—by theft.

Now, for a second time, Jacob was asking for a blessing. "Give me a blessing, or I will not let you go!" Once again, he heard the same question: "Who are you? Give me your name." This time Jacob did not say Esau, as he had said the first time. This time he gave his true name: "My name is Jacob." To give his name was to speak of his past and of his deception. He received a blessing this time by being himself, by claiming his past and by claiming responsibility. To be blessed, to return home, Jacob had to give his name. He had to accept responsibility for who he was and what he had done....And, for this he was wounded forever.

And yet, giving his real name did not lead to death as he had thought it would. He was not destroyed; he was wounded. As a matter of fact, he was changed. Because he had given his name and acknowledged his brokenness, Jacob was able to find his way home—not as an innocent person, not as a good person, but as one who had seen God face-to-face, had seen himself face-to-face...and yet had been spared. Jacob had wrestled in the night. He had wrestled with his sinfulness, his brokenness, and his lostness. In claiming his own self and responsibility for himself, he did not find obliteration as he had thought he would. Instead, he found the way home. He found mercy and forgiveness.

Jacob's struggle to go home is instructive to those of us who have accepted the identity of being white. It is a name borne in deception and theft. We have created the system of race to maintain that deception and theft. We have created a false name for ourselves. Just as Jacob took the false name Esau to receive a blessing, so we also have taken the false name white to receive material blessings. We who have renamed ourselves white have received great benefits from our deception. Yet, like Jacob, we have fled from our own identity most of our lives. Now we have the possibility of going home. There is no shortcut home. To go home, we first must pass through the land of our brothers and sisters—the kin whom we have cheated and crushed, the people of darker color. The land of Esau is the land of equality for us.*

To find our home, we must lift up our deception and acknowledge our relationship to our brothers and sisters whom we have cheated. We must acknowledge our equality and our common destiny as members of the same human family. This is painful. It is not easily accomplished. We who claim "whiteness" continue to avoid a genuine encounter at almost any cost. There is no going home without this encounter, however. It simply cannot be done without passing through the land of equality, that sense of brotherhood and sisterhood and common ground with people of darker color which we have so long denied and from which we have fled. It will be painful, but we will not be destroyed, as the story of Esau and Jacob suggests.

Who will we be if we pass through Esau's land, the land of equality, and find our real identity? Who will we be if we find that we are first of all people, not white people? We have many names—Irish, Italian (it took them a while to become "white"), Scottish, French, Belgian, and many others, including many mixtures thereof. Rather than white Americans, we can remember that we are people with many heritages who have come to a new land and society. There are great possibilities in this process, the possibilities of recreating an understanding of life built on the models of a tapestry of common humanity and cooperation instead of the model of a race and a competition in which some are destined to win and some are destined to lose. We cannot go home—any of us, all of us—until we have reclaimed our common humanity and our kinship.

We also can seek to recover the history of those classified as white who have sought to reject that identification in various ways. There have been white people who have labored against the system of race throughout this nation's history, but we have

---

* I am indebted for this insight to Ed Loring of the Open Door Community in Atlanta.

forgotten most of their names. We need to recover those names and those stories so that we who have been deemed white can begin to find another identity.

There were families identified as white on the Underground Railroad, as well, who hid people treated as slaves as they fought to find freedom.* Our society has forgotten many of their names, also, for they were not acting white. In *The Underground Railroad* (New York: Simon and Schuster, 1987) Charles L. Blackson describes the Coffin family in North Carolina who began as early as 1819 to hide and conduct people called slaves who were fleeing for freedom. Vestal Coffin organized the Underground Railroad near Guilford College in 1819. His son Addison joined as a youth and continued into old age, and Vestal's cousin Levi started in his youth and later moved to Indiana to provide a way station there (pp. 61-62). Abby Kelley shocked people when she combined her fight for women's rights with a fight for equal rights for black people. Feminists Lucy Stone, Susan B. Anthony, and Elizabeth Cady Stanton learned at her feet. Her witness was so strong that these words were lifted up at her funeral in 1887:

> Few Americans can be named—statesmen, scholars, orators, no matter how gifted—who did so much for the abolition of American slavery as did the woman whose worn-out frame lies before us. She was one of the few—the marked few—whose words startled and aroused the land; who compelled attention (and that not by mere vehemency of speech, but by genuine earnestness of heart and soul); who made the guilty tremble; who forced sleeping consciences to awake, and forbade that they should sleep again until slavery ceased.
>
> There were indeed other women who early and late befriended the slave's cause. But that cause could not have gone forward as it did, but for Abby Kelley Foster. No one of them ever did take, ever could have taken the place she so marvelously filled; could ever have done the amount of

---

* I am indebted to David Billings of the People's Institute in New Orleans for this insight.

telling, incisive, incessant work which she did for so many years; work so laborious, persistent, continuous, undismayed, as most persons now would pronounce impossible, and as most men, of however sturdy make, could not have been able to endure (Dorothy Sterling, *Ahead of Her Time: Abby Kelley and the Politics of Antislavery* [New York: W. W. Norton, 1991], pp. 386-387).

Still others seen as white fought hard for equality during Reconstruction and its aftermath. The stories of these white people who sought to reject the system of race await our rediscovery. Their stories tell us that the system of race is not rooted in inexorable reality but in a system of deception and oppression, a system that was chosen and created. Their stories tell us that it is possible to fight against one's identity as white and stand against the system of race.

This century has seen many white people who have fought for equality. Myles Horton was cofounder of The Highlander Center in Tennessee, where Martin Luther King, Jr., Rosa Parks, and many others prepared for the struggle in the civil rights movement. Anne Braden of the Southern Organizing Committee in Kentucky has been relentless in her work against racism. Clarence Jordan cofounded the Koinonia community in south Georgia in the 1940s as a place where black and white people could live and work together.

My contemporary and childhood friend David Billings is a United Methodist minister in New Orleans who continues to challenge me and others as a core trainer for the People's Institute for Survival and Beyond. His spouse Margery Freeman is also a trainer for the People's Institute and has long been involved in antiracist training in public education. Ed Loring and Murphy Davis are cofounders of the Open Door Community in Atlanta, a residential community of Christians called to ministry with the homeless poor and prisoners. They are both Presbyterian ministers and have long been witnesses for the connection between racial classification and homelessness and our use of prisons. John and Dee Cole Vodicka of the Prison and Jail Project in Sumter County in south Georgia are doing stunning work in reeducating us all on the continuing power of the system of race in the jails and prisons of that area.*

There are, of course, many African-American people who are witnesses against the power of racism. I am grateful to them for their continuing refusal to be defined by race. I have named white people because we are not expected to struggle against race. These names remind us that there are white witnesses against the power of race, many more than I have named. Challenged by people of darker color, emboldened and encouraged by the Holy Spirit, and willing to risk exposing their own racism, these people and many others tell us that while the system of race is powerful, it is not the final word. The diversity God has created is not a problem. It is an opportunity, and these witnesses call on us to join them in this journey. It is the only way home.

The peril in which we all live cannot be overstated. We live in a dangerous time, when the system of race is seeking to regain its strength. If it does, it will threaten not only our society but the entire global community. There are no longer isolated nations, societies, or cultural tendencies. Unless we can gather the courage to face our own dependence on the system of race, we face immense danger. There have been witnesses for justice, equality, and freedom. Those witnesses are in our midst now. We are called to hear them, to listen to them, to be transformed by them, and to begin to be witnesses ourselves—all of us, whether the system of race calls us white, black, Asian, Hispanic, Native American, or other. Now is the time we must seek to join that great cloud of witnesses who have gone before us, who call us even now to come and be part of a heritage worthy of

---

* See Myles Horton, The Long Haul—An Autobiography (New York: Doubleday, 1990); "Anne Braden: Southern Activist," Steve Suitts, *Southern Changes*, Spring, 1993, pp. 13-16; and Clarence Jordan, *The Substance of Faith and Other Cotton Patch Sermons* (New York: Association Press, 1972). For information on The People's Institute for Survival and Beyond, contact them at 1444 N. Johnson Street, New Orleans, LA 70116. Contact The Open Door at 910 Ponce de Leon Avenue, N.E., Atlanta, GA 30306. Contact the Prison and Jail Project at 1324 Highway 49 South, Americus, GA 31709.

humanity. The task is immense and may seem overwhelming, but the witnesses call to us. There are possibilities for movement and change, and there is hope. We now turn to one such model—Oakhurst Presbyterian Church—which demonstrates both the struggles and the hopes that are encountered when we wrestle with the demon of race.

CHAPTER 10

"Many Streams, One River"

From many threads, one tapestry.
From many streams, one river.
We are Oakhurst.

They stand in front of the curtain in the fellowship hall of Oakhurst Presbyterian Church on a Sunday morning. On cue, they begin singing at our Sunday school kick-off rally. They dance, roll their arms, and giggle as they sing "Jesus is the rock who rolls my blues away," a song they learned together at church camp the previous summer. We have nicknamed them the "Supremes" after the famous 1960s singing group. Their names are Noelle, a fifth grader whose parents were born in Jamaica; Tiffany, a sixth grader whose parents are African-American; and my daughter, Susan, a sixth grader of European ancestry. They are part of the vision and hope of Oakhurst.

On another occasion, the sanctuary is filled to overflowing. It is a sad and mournful time, the funeral of a young African-American woman who died of a rare blood disease. She was an outstanding teacher and left behind a teen-age son at her death. Two women, one white and one black, sing together of sorrow and thanksgiving for the life and work of our departed sister, taken so early from us. At the close of the service, a lone dancer steps forward, a young African-American woman who had been a student of the sister who passed. Dressed all in black, she dances to the song "To Be Young, Gifted, and Black"; and as she

147

moves across the front of the sanctuary, she addresses the coffin. She doesn't plead with the coffin—she slaps it! She slaps it to express our anger at the loss. She slaps it to give thanks for the life of our sister. She slaps it to tell death that there is a "great gettin' up mornin,'" to tell death that its power is not final or domineering. The gift of life and the gift of love that we know through God is the center of all that exists.

This is our life at Oakhurst Presbyterian Church. We are a multicultural church of 160 members, split about evenly between black people and white people. We seek to be faithful to the proclamation that Jesus Christ has broken down the barriers of the world. Although we are a long way from the glory land, we are seeking to be realistic about the power of race, and we are attempting to live the truth that the Gospel is more powerful than the idols of the world. A study by Emory University described us as follows:

> "Multi-racial, Forward-thinking, Biblically-based, Jesus-centered" reads the advertisement for Oakhurst Presbyterian Church which ran in the Atlanta *Constitution-Journal* in the weeks leading up to the congregation's seventieth anniversary celebration in the fall of 1991. All four of the claims made by the advertisement are true: the church's multi-racial character can be seen at a glance at any gathering; it is "forward-thinking" as it seeks to be a different kind of community working deliberately for a more just society; the goals it espouses and the metaphors it uses to describe its life and mission are explicitly drawn from scripture; and its Jesus-centeredness can be heard in its proclamation and witness to "the good news of Jesus Christ" from day to day, week to week, and year to year (Chuck Foster, Candler School of Theology, Emory University, Atlanta, 1992, p. 104).

We are a community of faith on a journey with God. Like the people of Israel brought out of slavery to journey with God, we often are grumpy and often long for a return to less complicated places and times. Yet, God continues to push us and pull us, and there are times when we can see and experience the Promised

Land. I offer our story as a resource for reflection and a source of hope for those who feel overwhelmed by the power of race. I am grateful to the Session of Oakhurst, our local governing body, for agreeing to allow me to share our story.

We have not always been multiracial. For most of its life, Oakhurst Presbyterian Church was a white, neighborhood-based congregation. The movement of the city changed its life significantly. In the "urban renewal" program of the 1960s in this country, African-Americans were displaced from their homes; this happened in Atlanta also. When their homes were taken from them in Atlanta, African-Americans moved into south Dekalb County, just east of the city of Atlanta. Their relocation included the Oakhurst neighborhood, and this began the dramatic shift that has been repeated many times in this country: white people fleeing from people of darker color.

Oakhurst Church began in September 1921, as a white, working-class church in Decatur, a small town older than Atlanta, in whose shadow it now sits. From the denomination's point of view, it was a successful church. At its twenty-fifth anniversary in 1946, it had seven hundred members; by 1960, it had reached almost 900 members. It had also grown from a church with a blue-collar nucleus to a prosperous middle-class church. It served regularly as host for graduation services for Columbia Theological Seminary, a nearby Presbyterian seminary. It was the kind of church in which our denomination and our Presbytery took pride. Though its members had been nurtured in the racism of the times, it was soon to encounter the challenge of the system of race head-on.

As Mary Esther Porter has pointed out (unpublished thesis, Emory University, 1992), the civil rights movement came to Atlanta when the white membership of Oakhurst began to wrestle with its response. In November 1963, the church's governing body, the Session, debated whether it would allow all persons to come to worship, "regardless of race or color." After much debate in the Session and in the congregation, a policy of open seating was finally adopted. Less satisfactory was a 1964 decision about opening the upcoming Vacation Bible School to all—the Session decided to send any black children who came to Oakhurst to the *black* Presbyterian church in Decatur.

These decisions reflected the struggle of the white leaders and members at Oakhurst. While wanting to affirm the theoretical principle of equality of all before God, they could hardly bring themselves to affirm it in the daily activities of the church. Soon it would come face-to-face with the power of race in a process that almost all its members had feared. African-American people began to move into the neighborhood. It was one thing to begrudgingly welcome black people to worship; it was quite another to live next door. Oakhurst was a neighborhood church, and when white flight began in the neighborhood, its membership plummeted.

The Session and the congregation faced a difficult situation. White people who were members began to flee from the neighborhood. Some returned to worship, but most did not return and soon transferred their membership to other churches in "safer," all-white neighborhoods. The Session considered a recommendation to close the church doors. After all, other Presbyterian churches in similar situations were closing and selling their buildings to black congregations. The Session, refusing to move and close its doors, decided to stay.

The first African-American member, Nate Mosby, came to Oakhurst in 1969 and joined in 1970. As he is fond of saying, "After I joined the church, its membership increased rapidly from 800 to 200!" The decline in membership continued until it reached its low point of 80 members at the end of 1982. Yet, during these years, the church did not close down and did not flee, as other neighborhood churches have done and continue to do throughout this country. While it was demoralized and struggling, the congregation tenaciously held on. Its spirit during these years is perhaps best captured in words from its Mission Statement, adopted in September 1990:

> Oakhurst Presbyterian Church is a community of diversities. We come from different places, from different economic levels, from different countries of the world. We are a church in the city. Our life has known the movement of the city: we were once all of one kind. Then our church became multi-racial and felt small and insignificant. And our people were afraid, afraid of ourselves from different

races, afraid of ourselves from different cultures. The faithfulness of those who stayed and those who came gave us courage. By God's power we have been given grace through what we thought was our weakness. In the midst of our fears God has surprised us and blessed us. The diversity which we feared has empowered us to confront God's truth in the world. In Jesus Christ the dividing walls of hostility have been broken down. Though we are born into diverse earthly families, our life together at Oakhurst has led us to affirm that we are called to be one family through the life, death and resurrection of Jesus Christ.

During these difficult years, Oakhurst was blessed with fine ministerial leadership: Jack Morris, Lawrence Bottoms, and Bruce Gannaway. Jack Morris, who is white, recruited the first black members to Oakhurst; he and his wife, Joy, challenged the church to institute programs for the new neighbors. Lawrence Bottoms was a giant in the former southern Presbyterian church, an African-American who endured many indignities yet remained a powerful witness. During his pastorate at Oakhurst, he was elected the first and only African-American moderator of the Presbyterian Church in the United States, prior to its merger with the United Presbyterian Church in 1983. He gave legitimacy to Oakhurst's experiment of being a white church seeking to stay in a neighborhood that was changing because of white flight.

Bruce Gannaway and his wife, Ollie, had been white missionaries in Africa and thus brought an international view of race. Through their hard work, they were successful in recruiting strong black leaders in the community to this strange white church. Through God's leading, they helped lay the foundation for the future. It was a difficult process: Many whites continued to leave, few new whites came, and the membership continued to drop until it had lost 91 percent of its membership over two decades.

Oakhurst had barely survived. When I came to visit the church in the fall of 1983 to see if Oakhurst and I wanted to pursue the possibility of my being called as pastor there, it was a demoralizing time. As I toured the building, the host had a huge ring of keys; every door inside and out seemed to be locked. Oakhurst had survived, but it felt like a fortress under siege. And yet, it *had* stayed and had some life. There was hope—hard to see and even harder to feel, but some hope, nonetheless.

Oakhurst asked me to be its pastor in December 1982. I was interested, but I was reluctant. It seemed so depressing and so overwhelming, and I sensed that great loneliness awaited me. My wife, Caroline Leach, is also a Presbyterian minister, but she was not being called there as pastor because she wanted to stay home a bit longer with our small children. (I had hopes of her eventually serving as pastor there, and later in 1984 she did become the associate pastor.) After much prayer and discussion, I decided to accept the call to become the eleventh pastor of Oakhurst. We arrived in February 1983 and began a long and astonishing journey.

When worshipers now enter the sanctuary at Oakhurst, they are struck by a huge stained glass window at the back of the choir loft. It depicts the Ascension of Jesus, and it has graced the sanctuary for almost fifty years. In 1989 we made a dramatic change in this window. We changed the depiction of Jesus from a European, white figure to a brown-skinned figure that looks like a Mid-East Jew, which Jesus was. We also changed the portrayal of the disciples who watched Jesus ascend to heaven. We included two "nappy-headed" men and a woman in the group of disciples. This change was difficult. One of our most faithful white members felt saddened that the white heritage could not be accepted.

Yet, white heritage remains at Oakhurst. At the other end of the sanctuary is a white Jesus, and thus worshipers at Oakhurst see at least two images of Jesus. I often stand in the aisle of the sanctuary for the pastoral prayer, positioning myself between the two images of Jesus. I had not realized the physical significance of this until it was noted in the Emory University study of our congregation.

> In the weekly repetition of this ritual act in worship, Marshall McLuhan's insight that the "medium is the message" underscores and reinforces the verbal messages of the

people. As Nibs stands at the center of their common life and gathers up and restates congregational concerns and joys so that everyone can hear, the solidarity of those present is intensified. At the same time, his physical position between the black and white stained glass images of Jesus underscores the reality of the tensions people experience in the relationship of the races in a southern city. The persistent interplay of these experiences of solidarity and daily encounters with the hostilities that divide people from each other illumine the pervasive sense of hope that informs congregational life in the midst of a profoundly realistic assessment of the many barriers to the quality of relationships envisioned by St. Paul for Christian community (p. 14).

There have been dramatic and heartening changes at Oakhurst. It was a strong, powerful church that had neglected to notice how dependent it was on the system of race. When the congregation came face-to-face with the system of race, it was severely injured. When it had to acknowledge the importance of its racial identity as white, it crumbled. Many white members fled rather than stay and struggle with the system of race. Those few whites who stayed wanted to retain their power and to remake the African-Americans into their image. And, yet through God's power, the church made the transition from *being dependent* on the system of race to *confronting* the system of race. Its membership increased to 160 by the end of 1994, and its community ministry blossomed and is now booming. The change in its sense of self is seen in another part of its Mission Statement.

Worldly differences fail to separate our folk. Instead, these differences are the threads that the love of Jesus Christ weaves into one tapestry—Oakhurst Presbyterian Church. We are young woven with old, black with white, male with female. We are employed woven with unemployed, poor with comfortable, strong with broken. We are courageous woven with disheartened, able with sick, hurt with healers. The world uses these categories to separate people from one another and to erect barriers between people. Our life together at Oakhurst Presbyterian Church, however, is a proclamation that people are more than just race, gender and economic class. We all find dignity at Oakhurst no matter the category in which society places us. And we celebrate that each difference finds its beauty and its strength in the Oakhurst tapestry.

Though we have a long way to go, we have made significant progress in affirming diversity and confronting the system of race. The Reverend Joan Salmon-Campbell, the African-American moderator of our denomination in 1989, had these words to say about Oakhurst in a sermon she preached in our church.

It has been a long, long time since I have worshipped in a congregation quite like this one. I celebrate who you are. I dare say you are one of the best kept secrets in the entire denomination, for rarely do I see a congregation so diverse, as you represent so many different kinds of people. Rarely am I in the midst of God's people who bother to take the time to hear the concerns of the people in the pew and then intentionally lift them up before the Lord and rejoice. I thank God for you and the privilege of being in your midst this morning.

What happened? What enabled this congregation, which had been so defined by the system of race, to shift from that definition? What empowered this congregation to be able to confront its definition by race and challenge that definition in its own life and in the life of the world?

The process of transformation did not begin in 1983. It began when God called Oakhurst into being, and it continues through the faithfulness of God and the faith of God's people at Oakhurst. Stumbling and bumbling, maddened at times, saddened at times, discouraged and yet faithful, Oakhurst has been transformed through the power of God. Although we continue to have struggles and difficulties, the steps in our journey thus far can be helpful to those whose hearts grow faint as the system of race regains its power and threatens to overwhelm us.

The first step for this congregation was to acknowledge and proclaim the reality that God is the center of our lives. Since we are a Christian church, this step involves the proclamation of God's unique revelation in Jesus Christ. This faith puts God above all else in our lives—money, gender, race, and nationality are all lesser entities. This faith enabled the small group of white people at Oakhurst to stay as the congregation shrunk and black people came to worship. As white friends departed, few white folk replaced them; there was discouragement and a deep sense of loss. Their belief that God was calling them to this ministry enabled the whites to persevere. This faith enabled the black people to stay, even after receiving all kinds of messages that their identities and their culture were not particularly welcome at Oakhurst. Their music was belittled, their input was depreciated, and their souls were hungry; but this sense of being called by God enabled the black people to hold fast at Oakhurst.

This first step depends on the affirmation of God's love for us—each of us and all of us. We lift up the Good News that God's love is deep and broad, and it defines our lives. God is the meaning and the source of our lives. We emphasize this again and again and again. The Good News is this: We are given life by God; we are given meaning by God; we belong to God.

On one level, this is astonishingly good news! No matter what the world tells us, no matter what the world does to us, we belong to God. Our ultimate destiny belongs to God. As Presbyterians, we also affirm John Calvin's sense of the chief purpose of human life: to glorify God and enjoy God forever. Enjoy God? What kind of talk is that from Christians, especially Presbyterians, who are often called the "frozen chosen?" This sense of celebration is one of the great gifts that African-Americans bring to American religious life, a sense of God's presence that is enjoyable, not oppressive. For most white Americans, religion is oppressive and repressive. God is out to crush us, and unless we crush ourselves, God will get us. For many African-Americans, God is life-giving and life-sustaining. Rather than being out to get us unless we do right, God is seen as the One who enables us to make it through this life. Rather than being the terrible, angry deity that most white Americans have emphasized, God is seen by African-Americans as the One who gives life and who gives meaning. When our Sanctuary Mass Choir sings from the African-American tradition, "God is the meaning and the source of my life," it is a powerful affirmation that God is able to sustain us and bring us through the storms of life. This affirmation is sung not when people are powerful and wealthy and feeling in control but when people are poor and being crushed and feeling oppressed.

This sense of enjoying God does not mean that God is seen as a permissive sugar daddy who says yes to everything and everybody. The crucifixion is central to African-Americans because they know the power of humanity's "No," which the crucifixion represents. The crucifixion speaks loudly and clearly about the cost of human sinfulness, injustice, and idolatry. To see God as life-sustainer does not mean a negation of the crucifixion. It means a deeper understanding that the crucifixion is not the bribe of an angry judge ready to crush us. It means that the crucifixion is seen as a sign of the depth of God's love for us: "While we were yet sinners, Christ died for us" (Romans 5:8) and echoed in John's Gospel: —"God sent the Son into the world not to condemn the world, but that the world through Him might be saved" (John 3:17).

God actively engaging us in this life, like the woman who turns over the furniture in her house in search of that one small lost coin, like the father who welcomes back his prodigal son— this is the God we know in the Good News of Jesus Christ. This is what we emphasize at Oakhurst. This God is at the center of our lives, looking for us, guiding us, pulling us back on the path, carrying us, challenging us, loving us. We hear that we are defined, first and foremost, as children of God. Though economic class, gender, skin color, sexual orientation, nationality, and other lesser powers want to claim ultimacy in our lives, we are reminded constantly that God is our central definition. We are sustained in this life by that definition. One of our African-American grandmothers and I were discussing this definition in relation to her granddaughter, who has attended our church all of her young life. The grandmother was concerned because her black granddaughter seemed too comfortable around white people. She attributed this comfort to her granddaughter's being around white people at Oakhurst. She told me that one day she and her five-year-old granddaughter were in a mall when a white man bumped into the granddaughter and moved on without apologizing to her. The granddaughter turned to the man and said, "You forgot to say 'excuse me'." He paid no attention and kept on walking. The granddaughter ran up to him again, got his attention, and said again, "You forgot to say 'excuse me'." The white man then apologized.

My friend told me this story as an example of what had happened to her granddaughter in our biracial church. She had encountered white people as human beings, and now she expected all white people to receive her as a human being. She had lost sight of the system of race, and it was dangerous to do that. I was reminded once again of this terrible dilemma in which the system of race places African-American people: Deny your humanity in the white world or get hurt.

As we discussed the situation, however, it became clear that the decision for African-American people is not whether to avoid the hurt, because they have little choice. The system of race will hurt African-American people—there is no way around that. The decision for African-American people is how to receive the hurt. We both agreed, reluctantly and sadly, that we preferred that the granddaughter be hurt by her strength rather than by turning the process inward and accepting the white definition of herself. To affirm her humanity in the white world will inevitably lead to hurt and rebuttal by the white world. To deny her humanity in the white world would be a deeper hurt: It would allow the system of race to define her. The question is not how to avoid the pain, but how to prepare for the pain and use it as an instrument of growth rather than an instrument of self-destruction. We both agreed that Oakhurst was a place where her granddaughter could hear the Good News that she was somebody and prepare for the pain.

On another level, however, the emphasis that we are defined primarily by God is disturbing. Those of us who are comfortable, and especially those of us who are white, hear this primary definition as bad news. It is bad news because we are asked to hear the extent to which we have accepted the definition of lesser powers in our lives. At Oakhurst, some white people hear this Good News as bad news because they hear it as antiwhite.

The affirmation that our central definition is a child of God is perceived as being subversive to being defined as white. In this sense, their reaction is correct. We are asking ourselves at Oakhurst to reconsider our primary definition, whether that definition is skin color or economic status or whatever. If our primary definition of ourselves is whiteness, then we will be asked to reconsider. As we have seen in this book, most of us who are white do not think about our definition. Yet, when it is revealed how important our racial classification is to us and to this society, the reaction is anger, irritation, and guilt. Many of our white folk, then, must go through a painful process of reconsidering how important our whiteness is to them.

It is in this sense that good news becomes the bad news. All of us stand in need of repentance—and for those of us who are white, it is a double dose of difficulty. Not only do we have to reconsider our own idolatry, but we also have to reconsider how much we have assigned responsibility for the problems of race to black people. We hear that it is those of us who are white who have created and maintain the system of race. We have to re-orient the way we look at ourselves and the way we look at people of darker color.

God at the center of our lives is Good News for us at Oakhurst. For those of us who can respond to this proclamation, there is a great gift waiting. It is a gift that enables us to receive our true humanity as a child of God and to see others as children of God, first and foremost. It is a gift that enables us to celebrate our unity as children of God. It is a gift that enables us to celebrate our diversity of skin colors, languages, and heights (I am short, so I especially like this one!). Diversity becomes a gift, not a problem.

This emphasis on the nature of diversity is the second step that Oakhurst has taken in an effort to become a multicultural congregation. God is at the center of life and that God has created diversity. This second step affirms that God intends for us to build community on that diverse foundation. Diversity is often seen as a problem in our culture rather than as an opportunity; and as long as diversity is seen as a problem, we will seek to flee from it. What if we saw diversity in a new light? Rather than perceiving it as a problem, what if we saw it as an opportunity for learning more about God's love and an opportunity for sharing the news of God's love? This second step sounds simple but is yet profound. Only our perceptions change—nothing changes and yet everything changes.

We have sought to affirm this sense of diversity in several ways. We affirm it in public, even nationally, as heard on a segment of National Public Radio's "All Things Considered":

Oakhurst Presbyterian Church is unremarkable on the outside, but the congregation inside is quite remarkable.... people from the most divergent backgrounds—middle class professionals, blue collar and pink collar workers, welfare recipients, old, young, and very young, black, white, Asian, gay and straight. All seem to feel comfortable there, and speak their minds (April 10, 1994, Ted Clark reporting).

We affirm this in our worship life. Early on in our worship service, we have a time called the Ritual of Friendship, when people greet one another. It is not only turning in the pew to shake hands with a neighbor. It is a time when people get up and really greet one another, moving across the sanctuary to hug and shake hands and acknowledge one another. We came to this ritual by accident (or by God's grace). A white girl in the third grade, whose family worshiped with us while her mother was a seminary student, pointed out to me that in her former church, people stood up to greet one another instead of only turning to shake hands. I promised her that I would announce this opportunity the next Sunday, and the result amazed me. People not only stood up—they walked to other pews, sometimes from front to back, to greet other people. Isaiah 11 promises that a little child shall lead us, and in this case, she did. How often do the children lead us!

In this time of greeting, worship participants will touch someone of a different skin color and a different culture. We affirm the diversity that God has created in a concrete way—we touch the flesh of someone different from us, someone society has told us is our enemy. This greeting time can take several minutes, and it has lengthened our worship service. Initially, it elicited many complaints from both black and white people who considered it superfluous and even derogatory in worship. Those complaints have largely faded as the genuine warmth and power are felt in the greeting time. This affirmation of God's creation of diversity is now an integral part of our worship: We greet one another as the sisters and brothers that God made us, seeking to leave behind the power of the idols which tell us that our diversity is a problem, not a gift.

We affirm this diversity in church life together. For almost all of our prayers—whether it be the benediction at worship, the thanksgiving prior to a church supper, or an injunction for guidance in a committee meeting—we form a circle to hold hands. We once again touch the flesh of another, and we emphasize that the circle is not complete without all of God's people being there.

We affirm diversity not because we want to win points for being inclusive but because we believe that this diversity is a buffer against human arrogance. We believe that God has given us diversity to remind us that our particular history is both important and limiting. We must know our own stories of who we are and how we came to be. Without a sense of that story, we have no roots. In our distrust of diversity, in seeing diversity as a problem, we have come to believe that our story is *the* story. By emphasizing the gift of diversity, we lift up the sense that our story is only *part* of the story. The whole story is to be found in looking not only at our own experience but in considering the validity of the experiences of others. This approach does not lead to relativism, as so many white people seem to believe. This approach leads to a rich and deep sense of what it means to be human and created in the image of God.

These two steps have been essential in shifting Oakhurst from a congregation centered on race to a congregation seeking to challenge the system of race. A third step—to acknowledge the continuing power of race in our lives, as individuals, families, and as a congregation—is also necessary. In our worship service, our usual procedure is to move into a time of confession after the ritual of friendship, which acknowledges the identity God has given us. The time of confession acknowledges the definition that we have given ourselves. We acknowledge in the greeting that God has broken down the barriers of the world in Jesus Christ. We acknowledge in the confession that we are steadily building them back up. We emphasize this because white people especially want to skip over racism. We want to believe that going to a seminar, reading a book, or coming to worship at Oakhurst will enable us to be rid of the system of race. Would that worship at Oakhurst or anywhere else were that life-changing!

Our life at Oakhurst acknowledges how central "race" and other idols continue to be to its individual members and to its life as a congregation. We celebrate diversity, but we also recognize how difficult it is to appropriate that gift in a culture where race is central. In any attempt to deal with the power of race, both the vision of diversity and the reality of racism must be kept before us at all times.

One of our most important decisions early in my tenure at Oakhurst emphasizes this. When I came to Oakhurst as pastor, our choir director was a white seminary student from Candler School of Theology at Emory University. He was an excellent director; but his time as a student came to an end, and he accepted a call to be a pastor at another church. Our choir director's position thus became vacant, and we began to search for a replacement. Our search committee was diverse and was headed by a white woman, who is a skilled musician and former music teacher.

We interviewed several candidates, and the clear choice to us on the search committee was an African-American who had great skills on the organ and impeccable credentials. He could play and direct many kinds of music, and he had just left a wealthy and prestigious white congregation. Rather than feeling elated at such a possibility, I felt anxiety as we prepared to take a recommendation to the Session, our local church's governing body. The source of my anxiety was not the difficulty of finances but his skin color. Oakhurst had never had a black choir director.

The Session meeting demonstrated that my anxiety was not ill-founded. Ten of our twelve elders attended, six white and four black. In Presbyterian churches, the pastor is the moderator of the Session meetings and has a vote. The white woman who chaired the Search Committee made its report, recommending that we hire our first African-American choir director. We fielded many questions about his qualifications, his salary, and the type of music he would be playing. No one ever said: "I am uncomfortable with this recommendation because the proposed candidate is black." The closest we got to a comment on race were questions about the musical selections he would be making. None of the elders said, "I believe the reason for the hesitancy on this candidate is that he is black." As is so often the case in this society, we had a discussion where the issue of race was central but yet never mentioned directly. In this oblique manner, the elders circled one another without ever being direct about the central issue.

Whatever the intentions behind the questions, when it came time to vote, the intentions became clear. The first vote ended in a 5-5 tie, without my voting. The five voting against the recommendation were all white; the five votes for it included the four black elders and the white chair of the Search Committee. We voted a second time, with the same result; but this time, I cast the deciding vote for the recommendation. It carried 6-5; and by the slimmest of margins, one of the best organists and choir directors in the Atlanta area was hired at Oakhurst. It was a lesson in the vision of diversity and the reality of racism. There was also irony in this decision. As difficult as the decision was, none of us got exactly what we voted for! Our first African-American music director did not like gospel music, and his taste in music was closer to those white people who voted against his hiring than to those black people who voted for his hiring. It was as if God was laughing at us and poking fun at us as we struggled mightily with race, unable to name it but seeing it as central.

The discovery of humor is the final step in reorganizing ourselves at Oakhurst. There are lighter moments in our journeys in the wilderness land of race, moments that remind us of the absurdity of the system of race, moments that remind us not to take ourselves too seriously. Our son David was three years old when we came to Oakhurst. He has grown up there and is now fifteen years old. When he was little and learning to talk, he had not yet gotten the language of race. We have many visitors in worship at Oakhurst, and one day he was trying to describe one of the visitors. When we asked whether the visitor was white or black, he replied that the visitor was "plain." After much discussion, it became clear that "plain" was his word for what we call a white person. And, it seemed appropriate in more ways than one!

In making a speech recently, I quoted from the last speech of Malcolm X, the one quoted in Chapter 5, referring to the negative self-image many African-American people have of themselves: "We hated our heads, we hated the shape of our nose, we wanted one of those dog-like noses, you know...." I am not certain why it hit me at this particular point; but for the first time, I heard this description of me as a white person: "dog-nosed." I assume that I had been focusing so much on how well Malcolm had captured the negativity of being called black in this society, that I missed how well he had captured me: "dog-nosed." He may not be describing all white people, but he did describe me well. I have a large, long nose, just like my collie dog. Maybe it was my collie dog that triggered the recognition. He seems to be putting his nose in many places where he has no business putting it; but it is so long that it is difficult to keep him out, once he gets his nose in. Whatever the motivation, I was struck by the apt description "dog-nosed." Who would want a nose like mine, anyway?

Finally, I remember a moment in worship that is both priceless and powerful. One of our families includes four tow-headed, blond boys, the oldest our daughter's age. The youngest is perhaps the blondest of them all; and when Sunday school assignments were given to the children, he refused to accept his assignment because he would be separated from his two older brothers. The dark skinned African-American teacher of his older brothers graciously accepted him into her class, and he became one of her favorites. His family was absent from our church for a long while, and on their return to worship, this youngest boy spotted his teacher in the front part of the sanctuary. Without consulting anyone—indeed, without regard to other people's opinions—he went running down the aisle of the sanctuary to plant a big hug and kiss on his teacher to celebrate their reunion. In another context, this could have been the same old story of black women being adored by little white boys, but here it was genuine and moving. In a bold move with no forethought, the little boy had proclaimed that there are authentic moments when we join the work of Jesus Christ in breaking down the dividing walls of hostility; and he was received with joy by the elder who is his teacher.

The steps that we have discussed were and continue to be an integral part of our journey at Oakhurst. The appropriation of these steps was a process that scared us and made us hesitant. As we gained the courage to actually try them in our congregational life, we faced obstacles; but we also received gifts from God.

The obstacles were considerable. To seek to implement these steps meant significant shifts for both white and black people. For white folks, it meant acknowledging how much we had invested in the system of race. We felt that we should be given great recognition for staying in a changing neighborhood, that we had done something unnatural by staying. We stayed because we believed in the power of God and because we felt that these black folks needed our help. Our approach had been to develop community ministry programs, all of which were commendable and helpful. This approach assisted in covering one of the central dynamics of Oakhurst in this time of transition: White folk did not need to change. We rarely wanted to consider an agenda based on diversity—the idea that not only would black folk need to change but white folk might need to change also. In this sense, the white approach at Oakhurst was a traditional missionary posture—the white folks, who had the answers, would give the darker folk a great gift by staying in their presence and sharing the answers with them. We had to begin to hear that the darker folk might be able to help us as well.

For black folk, acknowledging these steps meant a tremendous step of faith. The white experience is that it is difficult for us to get to know black folk who often simply won't let us in. There is good reason for that protective distance—their experience with us has not been great. The best analogy I can give as a white person is the advice about snakes that I was given as a child. I was taught that if you encountered a snake, you should be very still and let the snake decide its course of action. So it is when black folks encounter what they fear—white folks. Unless they remain very still and quiet, they will likely get hurt. Whether they consciously express it or not, many black people have been taught to make white people feel comfortable by repressing their selves in the presence of white people. When we invited black people to join with us at Oakhurst, we were asking a lot. Undoubtedly, these questions and many more arose: Can white people really be in our presence? Can they deal with us as human beings? More importantly, can we deal with *them?* Can we be ourselves? Caroline and I experienced this process recently when we took a three-day trip with African-American members of our church and other African-American friends we did not know. As we ate together and played together, there was a growing sense of our common humanity. At the end of the trip, one of the African-American folks we had not known told us: "Ya'll really can hang, can't you?" It was an acknowledgment that they could be themselves, and we could, too, and that we all could survive the process of being ourselves in one another's presence!

At Oakhurst, we asked our black members not to be still and quiet but to push for a congregational agenda based on diversity. We also asked our white members to do the same. This was not as great a risk for whites, however, because we are accustomed to setting the agenda while not being required to pay a price. Black folk have not been accustomed to being welcomed to join in setting agendas for white folk. Their experience with whites is that seeking to set agendas for whites exacts a great cost. Yet, at Oakhurst, we asked our black members to risk this venture. Thanks to God's grace, many of them took the risk and have pushed the congregation for an agenda based on diversity rather than on the system of race.

What does an "agenda based on diversity" mean in practical terms? First, it means looking at our practice of worship. As in most congregations, worship is a central act, if not *the* central act. In our particular congregation, we looked at time allotted for worship, congregational participation, and music. Many white congregations must end their worship in an hour. Why? There is no good theological or ecclesiastical reason. What would it mean to let the elements of worship set the time rather than the time set the elements of worship? There was no significant discussion about this issue until the worship began to last beyond one hour. At that point, we got questions from both black and white members. Some white members saw no reason to worship longer than an hour. One black member said that she left the black church to come to Oakhurst to get away from an extended worship service. The concerns centered on two parts of the worship service. The first was the time used for greeting already discussed. This part was affirmed by our Session because it so strongly emphasizes that in worship God is reorienting our identities away from the barriers of the world.

The second part that elicited discussion about the length of worship is the time used for joys and concerns. On most Sundays, people are encouraged to stand up and verbally share joys or concerns for prayers. This exercise affirms unity and commonality in diversity—everyone gets sick, everyone has addicts in their acquaintance, everyone faces difficulties, everyone has moments of joy. It is an exercise in affirming the frailty, the humanity, and the possibility of all of our lives. Black people and white people who are concerned about being vulnerable to those of other races see their friends opening up. One of our black members told me that she could not believe that black people would share such things about their lives in front of white people. She thought that her brothers and sisters were crazy to do this. She, too, has changed to affirm this sharing as she has seen its power—she still doesn't share herself, however.

Our members find a source of deep and abiding meaning: The system of race does not have the final word. God's power does. They can share and feel welcomed into the tapestry of humanity that God has created. This sense of solidarity and community is seen in a letter written by one of our members to the national staff of our denomination:

> On one of my first Sundays at Oakhurst, an "older" African-American woman asked the pastor if she could share a song with the congregation during the time of "Sharing of Joys and Concerns." She walked to the front and sang in strong voice a song which she said the Lord had sent to her the evening before. The congregation was still and

quiet as they listened to the very real words of prayer which were sung from this woman's mouth.

She is one of the many reasons I chose to attend Oakhurst church. On my first Sunday at Oakhurst, I felt that I had "come home." There are no words which can fully describe the power and fellowship of prayer at Oakhurst Church. Personally, I can only describe the emotion.

My experience with prayer in the Presbyterian Church was a very traditional one. Growing up in a white Presbyterian church, prayer was silent and orderly. Prayer had focus and direction. Prayer was dignified and careful.

Her prayer was not silent or orderly. It was not focused or directed at a particular aim. Although it was dignified, it was not careful. Her prayer to the Lord was a testimony of her faith and belief in a God who had not ever left her side. As she sang, the power of her prayer brought the community of Oakhurst together as one people—listening to her song and truly feeling the presence of the Lord. I had never before experienced such an emotion.

The Sharing of Joys and Concerns at Oakhurst is truly a time of POWERFUL fellowship and prayer. It is a time when people from all walks of life can come together as a community and share in their pain and their fears; their joy and celebrations.

It is a time when a woman can stand up and ask for prayers as she goes through chemotherapy for breast cancer. It is a time when another can stand up and share her concerns for the neighborhood and for her children. It is a time when a man can stand and ask that we remember the people of Yugoslavia. It is a time when a mother can stand and tell about her son's successful athletic team and how proud she is of him. It is a time when a young child can stand up and ask for prayers for his father. It is a time when the congregation can cry together over the death of one of their members. It is a time when the congregation can rejoice together in the birth of a new baby (Letter from Rebecca Linafelt to Rev. James Andrews, April 21, 1993).

Selection of music for worship is always difficult, whatever the congregation. In a congregation as diverse as ours, it has been doubly difficult. Our response has been to develop two choirs, one that learns its music from the notes on paper and one that learns its music from the notes in the ears. Each has legitimacy and validity, and each choir is diverse in its membership. One choir will sing the beautiful anthem "In Remembrance of Me," accompanied by the organ and the plaintive notes of the recorder. Another choir will have us clapping our hands and tapping our feet to "Jesus, Won't You Come By Here" or "I Have So Much To Thank God For." This dual approach acknowledges that there is more than one kind of music and more than one way to praise God in music. Both blacks and whites have had to make adjustments. Perhaps the most telling moment was in a service when Dr. Joseph Lowery of the Southern Christian Leadership Conference was preaching in our worship. The gospel choir sang immediately before his sermon; the soloist was a young white woman. Dr. Lowery was stunned by her voice, and he shared with us his surprise and his delight: "I didn't know that white people could sing like that."

A second part of setting a congregational agenda based on diversity is to encourage discussions of diversity and of the continuing power of the system of race. Rather than fearing its power, we affirm the power of diversity; and we acknowledge the continuing power of race. We have a discussion group called the Oakhurst Supper Club that meets to discuss books, movies, and plays. This diverse group often has race and diversity at the center of its discussions. We meet in one another's homes; this provides another dimension of our experience together. It is rare that white people or black people go into one another's homes as peers. In our Supper Club, we do; and the social interaction that results is astonishing. We eat together, share ideas, and dispute one another's positions, and, in so doing, continue to deepen our awareness of one another's humanity.

We also have quarterly Oakhurst forums that lift up the dynamics of race and diversity. In one on "Race, Gender, and Sexual Orientation," the discussion was painful and heated, especially when the comparison was made between the treatment of homosexual people and the treatment of African-American people. Are they the same? Are they different? A white homosexual asserted that his sense of oppression was similar to the sense of oppression of an African-American. An African-American replied that there was a fundamental difference because homosexual persons could hide their sexual identity if they chose to do so—for black people, this was not an option. The point here was not to determine who was the most oppressed. The point was to attempt to open discussion. There was at least an opportunity for dialogue.

Early in 1994, we held a forum entitled "Guns, Jails, and Violence—What's Wrong with Us?" The "us" was deliberately kept vague because we know the societal pressure to say that it is the abnormality of black people that is the problem in relation to violence. Again, we had a difficult discussion, as our desire to limit and control black men began to become apparent. By "our desire," I do not mean just white people. "Our desire" refers to all of us—we have accepted the terrible lie that black men are the problem. These sessions often become tense because they expose the reluctance of both black and white folk to encounter and acknowledge the system of race in the presence of one another. Yet, we believe that this is an exercise that must be done because we avoid it so much in our culture.

The third part of setting an agenda based on diversity is the development of leadership in the congregation. We seek diversity in the membership, in our committees, and in our elders who govern the congregation. While we are not limited to the dreaded "quotas," we are always aware that a diverse group is stronger and wiser than a homogeneous group. White folk cannot speak for black folk, and black folk cannot speak for white folk. We acknowledge that as the current reality. We all long for the day when the power of the system of race will be broken, when people will be seen more as people of different colors in the rainbow rather than as black and white. That day has not yet come, and we would be foolish to pretend that it has. While we have a long way to go, significant leadership has emerged, both in relation to our congregation and the community at large.

One of our white families whose daughters went through a local, integrated school system has discovered a different reality as it shepherds two black girls through that same school system.

The family discovered that in one of the best public school systems in the state, an unofficial system of segregation targets the white youth for college and the black youth for other alternatives. This segregation has not been overt, but it is present and powerful nonetheless. Through the family's efforts and those of others, this situation has begun to shift in the school system. The family has learned some hard and difficult lessons as it finds a different approach this time, but it has been persistent and faithful in this task and has sought to open the eyes of others. It is a result of the family's being a part of Oakhurst.

One of our African-American elders, Azzie Preston, was part of a jury pool in a local county earlier this year. She was appalled to see the case of a thirteen-year-old African-American boy come to the court. He was being tried as an adult because he had robbed another African-American boy's pair of sneakers. There were extenuating circumstances; but for Azzie Preston, the situation was clear: The boy was being tried as an adult because he was black. She hoped to be selected for the jury, but she was not. She has led a fight to publicize this case, and she now is part of the steering committee to help defeat a change in Georgia's state constitution that would abolish much of the power of the parole board. Strengthened by Oakhurst, she has led a campaign to confront and to challenge racism in the judicial system, even as the white-controlled system proclaims its innocence, despite an incarceration rate for juveniles that is seventy-six percent black males (*Atlanta Constitution,* April 10, 1994, p. G-2). This is a sign of the development of her leadership capabilities through her leadership at Oakhurst.

In seeking to set our agenda based on diversity, we always return to the three important points: God's definition of us is primary, the diversity is a gift, and race has continuing power. God's definition of us gives us grounding and rootedness so that we are able to hear challenges and to grow. The idea of the gift of diversity continues to push us to see and hear one another as human beings, each unique despite our status as white or black. As we learn to hear one another, to listen and speak to one another as human beings, we are able to see that not all black people are alike and not all white people are alike. There are important cultural differences between blacks and whites, and we look to gain insights from both and from other cultures.

In the midst of this affirmation of the gift of diversity, we are always aware of the power of race. We tend to judge one another as white or black. To paraphrase St. Paul, if we believe that we are beyond the power of race, we deceive ourselves and add to its power. We will not soon reach the point where we do not see skin color first. It will be a given in our society and in our church for some time to come. To acknowledge this is not to be pessimistic or race-oriented. It is simply to acknowledge a system that operates best when it is not acknowledged. Just as the Gerasene man was healed by Jesus when his demon was named, so it is with race. It is only in naming it that there can be healing.

These are the essentials of the Oakhurst story. We offer the story as a guide, and as a source of hope. We have many miles to go at Oakhurst, but we are on the road. On the Sundays when our Sanctuary Mass Choir sings, we close the worship by joining hands and making a circle around the sanctuary. Our Mass Choir Director, JoAnn Price, leads us as we sing "There's a Sweet, Sweet Spirit." As we sing "and for these blessings, we lift our hearts in praise," we all lift our enjoined hands in a sign of thanksgiving and of commitment to what God has done here at Oakhurst. As we conclude this benediction in worship, we do indeed feel "that without a doubt we'll know, that we have been revived when we shall leave this place" ("There's a Sweet, Sweet Spirit," Doris Akers, Manna Music, 1962). It is rare that people are not moved by this singing and by this expression of solidarity across racial categories, flesh touching flesh and asking for God's Spirit to revive us. It is a recognition that, like death and taxes, race may always be with us in this culture; but it is also a recognition that through a willingness to engage pain and a willingness to listen, there are moments when we shall overcome.

We are on the road, and we invite you to join us as we seek to live the calling highlighted in the Emory study:

> Oakhurst Presbyterian Church is a radically multicultural community of faith. It challenges the assumptions of most Protestant church leaders that some degree of cultural,

economic, racial, and educational homogeneity is necessary if a congregation is to have a vital life and mission. It seeks to distribute power equitably among men and women, African American and European American. It values and brings together persons of all generations—young and old. These diverse persons are woven into one *"rainbow tapestry"* celebrated by the congregation and admired by the wider church. The congregation seeks to proclaim and witness to *"the good news of Jesus Christ"*—which takes concrete form in the tasks of breaking down the walls of hostility that divide people; gathering up diverse peoples into one family; confronting the powers and principalities that maintain structures of racism and injustice in contemporary systems and structures; discerning Christ in one's neighbor; and mediating the presence of Christ by pointing to and illuminating the sacred dimensions of daily experience.

Oakhurst has had to struggle to survive during the past twenty years. It continues to struggle to maintain its building. Yet we perceive that the strength and determination from these years of struggle, have nurtured a confidence in the membership to seek to pursue faithfully its resolute mission to proclaim through word and deed *"the good news in Jesus Christ"* (pp. 46-47).

We shall overcome. From many threads, one tapestry. From many streams, one river. We are Oakhurst. By God's grace, we are Oakhurst.

Recommended Readings

Bell, Derrick, *Faces at the Bottom of the Well: The Permanence of Racism in America* (New York: Basic Books, 1992). A bleak yet powerful view of the claim that racism is a permanent part of the American scene.

Bennett, Lerone, *Black Power, USA—The Human Side of Reconstruction, 1867-1877* (Baltimore: Penguin Books, 1967). A popular scholar has written a moving account of another side of Reconstruction from the black view.

Cone, James H., *Martin and Malcolm and America: A Dream or a Nightmare* (Maryknoll, NY: Orbis Books, 1991). One of the best analyses of the relationship of these two powerful leaders.

Davis, Angela T., *Women, Race, and Class* (New York: Vintage Books, 1983). A classic study of the intersection of these categories.

Edsall, Thomas Byrne and Mary D. Edsall, *Chain Reaction: The Impact of Race, Rights & Taxes on American Politics* (New York: W. W. Norton, 1990). This book examines the comeback of "race" as a motivator in political races. It provides stark clarity about the stunning Republican triumph in Congress in 1994.

Glasgow, Douglas G., *The Black Underclass: Poverty, Unemployment & Entrapment of Ghetto Youth* (New York: Vintage Books, 1981). A Howard University sociologist studied Watts ten years after the 1965 rebellion. Its analysis and insights are as contemporary as today's newspaper.

Hacker, Andrew, *Two Nations: Black and White, Separate, Hostile and Unequal* (New York: Scribner's, 1992). An examination of the influence of racial classification on contemporary problems. It focuses on the white approach to these problems.

Harding, Vincent, *Hope and History: Why We Must Share the Story of the Movement* (Maryknoll, NY: Orbis Books, 1990). The senior adviser to the PBS television series "Eyes on the Prize" challenges us to understand the importance of the civil rights movement.

hooks, bell, *Sisters of the Yam: Black Women and Self-Recovery* (Boston: South End Press, 1993). A book for the healing of black women but containing insight for us all.

Horton, Myles, *Long Haul: An Autobiography* (New York: Doubleday, 1990). The co-founder of Highlander (where Rosa Parks and Martin Luther King, Jr., trained for the movement) describes his journey as a white activist.

Jordan, June, *Technical Difficulties: African American Notes on the State of the Union* (New York: Pantheon, 1992). A collection of essays about the intersection of democracy, women's rights, and human rights. It contains one of the best essays on Martin Luther King, Jr., that I have ever read.

Kluger, Richard, *Simple Justice: The History of Brown v. Board of Education and Black America's Struggle for Equality* (New York: Vintage Books, 1975). A history of *Brown vs. Board of Education* from the post-Reconstruction onward.

Meier, August, *Negro Thought in America, 1880-1915* (Ann Arbor: University of Michigan Press, 1963). A classic study of the struggle of African-American people to respond to the monstrous growth of racism in these years.

Reagon, Bernice Johnson, *We Who Believe in Freedom: Sweet Honey in the Rock—Still on the Journey* (New York: Doubleday, 1993). The story of Sweet Honey in the Rock, a singing group born in the civil rights movement and that continues to combine music and human liberation.

Sojourners, "America's Original Sin: A Study Guide on White Racism," (Washington, D.C.: Sojourners Resource Center, 1992). A study guide for examining the roots and the continuing power of racism.

Sterling, Dorothy, *Ahead of Her Time: Abby Kelley and the Politics of Antislavery* (New York: W. W. Norton, 1991). A thorough biography of a forgotten giant of the abolitionist movement, with insight into the challenges posed by trying to combine women's rights and rights for people of darker color.

Wells, Ida B., *Crusade for Justice: The Autobiography of Ida B. Wells*, ed. Alfreda M. Duster (Chicago: University of Chicago Press, 1970). The autobiography of another civil rights movement giant who led the 1890s anti-lynching movement. Ida B. Wells was a fierce but loving warrior who refused to accept the anti-black rhetoric of American society.

Williams, Delores, *Sisters in the Wilderness: The Challenge of Womanist God-Talk* (Maryknoll, NY: Orbis Books, 1993). An exploration of the womanist African-American experience through the story of Hagar.

For training and education, the People's Institute for Survival and Beyond is the best resource group in the country. Contact them at 1444 North Johnson Street, New Orleans, Louisiana 70116.